THIS COMPREHENSIVE GUIDE IS AN EXCELLENT TOOL FOR ANYONE WANTING TO START AND SUSTAIN A WELL-RUN GALLERY. SANDRA BOWDEN AND MARIANNE LETTIERI HAVE EXTENSIVE KNOWLEDGE AND INSIGHTS THAT EVERY EXHIBITION MAKER NEEDS TO KNOW.

—*Stephen Childs, M.F.A.*
Los Angeles-based artist, educator, and Director of Exhibitions at Azusa Pacific University

ENGAGING ART AND FAITH IS ONE OF THE STRATEGIC AND BEAUTIFUL TASKS BEFORE THE CHURCH IN ITS MISSION IN THE TWENTY-FIRST CENTURY. THE EXHIBITS I'VE DONE WITH CIVA REPRESENT SOME OF THE HIGHLIGHTS OF MY CONGREGATIONAL MINISTRY OVER THE PAST TWENTY YEARS AS A PASTOR—THEY WERE ARTISTICALLY STUNNING AND SPIRITUALLY RENEWING. THIS HANDBOOK OUTLINES EXPERTLY HOW TO MAKE AN EXHIBIT AT YOUR CHURCH A SUCCESS.

—*Greg Cootsona, Ph.D.*
Pastor, educator, and author of *C. S. Lewis and the Crisis of a Christian*

I AM DEEPLY IMPRESSED BY THE DEPTH OF THIS DECEPTIVELY SIMPLE HOW-TO-GUIDE AND THE MATURITY OF ITS VISION. NO DOUBT THIS IS THE RESULT OF DECADES OF TRIAL AND ERROR ON THE PART OF MANY. WHAT IMPRESSES ME MOST IS WHAT THIS MOVEMENT IS MOTIVATED BY: THE INTEGRATION OF THE VISUAL ASPECT IN THE LIFE OF THE CHURCH, BE IT THE WORSHIP OF THE CONGREGATION, THE SPIRITUAL FORMATION OF ITS MEMBERS OR THE RELATIONSHIP WITH THE LARGER LOCAL COMMUNITIES.

—*Marleen Hengelaar-Rookmaaker*
International writer and commentator on liturgy and the visual arts, editor-in-chief of ArtWay.eu

ISBN:978-0-9706786-1-4

Any Internet addresses, product manufacturers, and organizations referenced in this book are offered as a resource. They are not intended to be or imply an endorsement by CIVA, nor does CIVA vouch for the content of these sites and addresses for the life of this book. All rights reserved. No part of this publication may be reproduced in any form or by any means without written consent of the copyright owners. Artworks in this publication are copyrighted by the artists or their agents.

IN APPRECIATION FOR UNDERWRITING THIS PROJECT

THE BOWDEN FAMILY FUND
THE TERRI D. BULLOCK FAMILY FOUNDATION
CARE | THE CENTER FOR THE ARTS, RELIGION AND EDUCATION
NORTHEAST INTERIOR SYSTEMS, INC.
MR. AND MRS. HOWARD AND CORRINNE RUSSELL

Printed in the United States of America by CIVA.

Published by CIVA | Christians in the Visual Arts   Copyright © 2015
CIVA is a non-profit charitable organization. Your tax exempt contributions support this publication and other CIVA projects. Additional copies of *Seeing the Unseen* may be purchased online at www.CIVA.org.

First Printing May 2015

SEEING THE UNSEEN

LAUNCHING AND MANAGING A CHURCH GALLERY

SANDRA BOWDEN   MARIANNE LETTIERI

CIVA

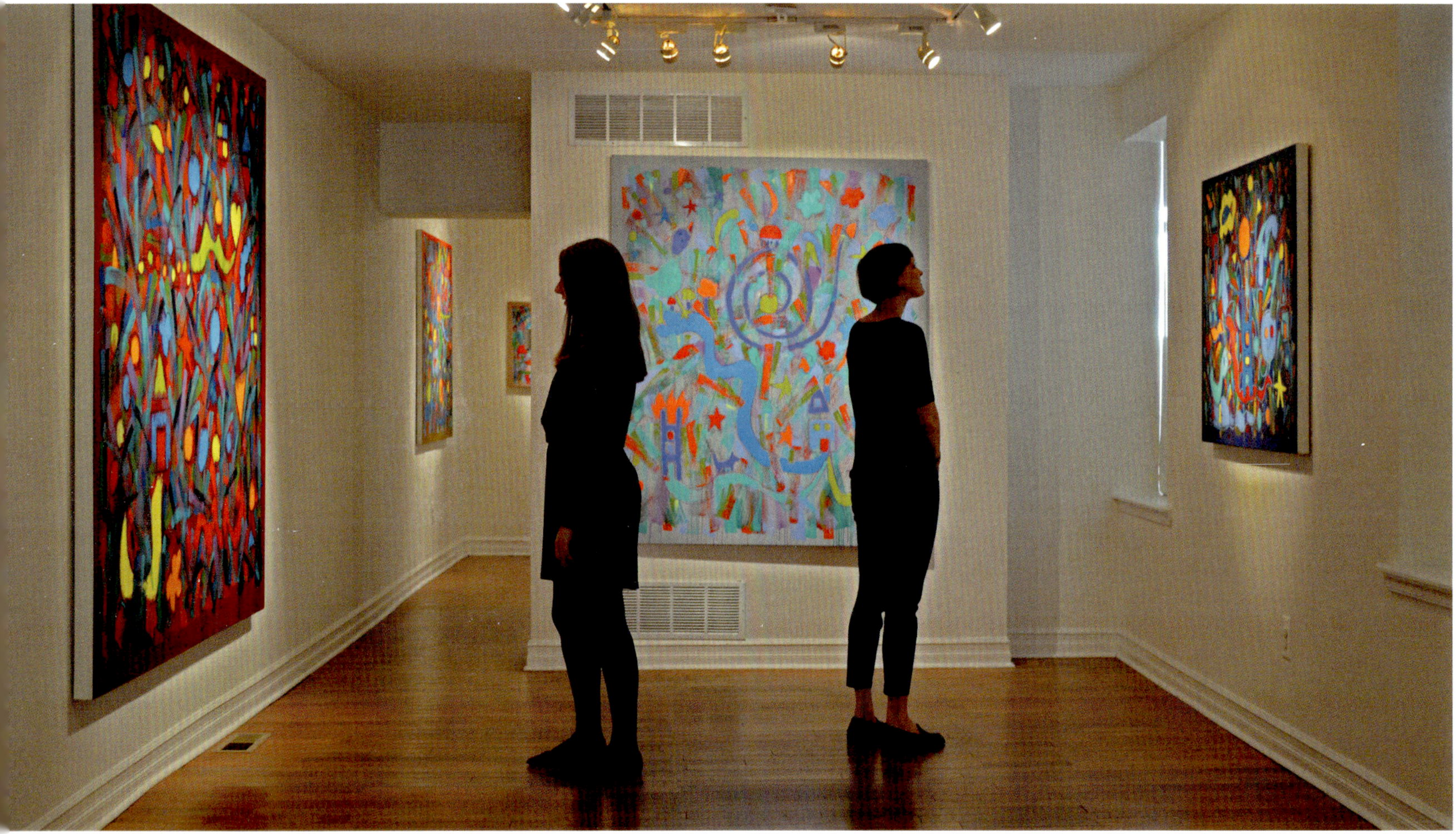

FOREWORD

INTRODUCTION

DEFINING THE GALLERY PROGRAM
1.1 VISUAL ARTS COMMITTEE
1.2 MISSION STATEMENT
1.3 GALLERY GOALS
1.4 GALLERY POLICIES

GALLERY MODELS
2.1 CONGREGATIONAL FOCUS
2.2 FAITH COMMUNITY FOCUS
2.3 PUBLIC FOCUS

DESIGNING THE GALLERY SPACE
3.1 WALLS, PARTITIONS, AND PANELS
3.2 HANGING SYSTEMS
3.3 LIGHTING FIXTURES AND WINDOWS
3.4 STORAGE

FUNDING THE GALLERY
4.1 CHURCH BUDGET ALLOWANCE
4.2 FRIENDS OF THE GALLERY
4.3 SPONSORS AND DONORS
4.4 GRANTS
4.5 AUCTIONS
4.6 ARTIST COMMISSIONS AND FEES
4.7 COLLABORATIONS AND CROWD FUNDING

BUSINESS ADMINISTRATION
5.1 SECURITY
5.2 INSURANCE
5.3 ARTIST HONORARIA
5.4 ARTIST LOAN AGREEMENT

PLANNING EXHIBITS
6.1 LENGTH AND FREQUENCY
6.2 CURATORIAL RESEARCH
6.3 THEMES AND MESSAGES
6.4 CONTROVERSY

KINDS OF EXHIBITS
7.1 ONE-PERSON
7.2 FROM THE CONGREGATION
7.3 HISTORICAL ART
7.4 THEMATIC
7.5 MEDIA-DRIVEN
7.6 OUTSIDE THE BOX

ORGANIZING JURIED SHOWS
8.1 TIMELINE
8.2 JURORS
8.3 PROSPECTUS
8.4 SELECTION PROCESS

HOW TO HANDLE ARTWORK
9.1 GENERAL GUIDELINES
9.2 RECEIVING, STORING, AND PACKING
9.3 MOVING ARTWORK
9.4 CONDITION REPORTS
9.5 WHEN DAMAGE OCCURS

INSTALLING EXHIBITS
10.1 ARRANGING ART
10.2 SPACING ART
10.3 HANGING ART
10.4 ADJUSTING LIGHTS
10.5 DOCUMENTING THE DISPLAY

ENGAGING VIEWERS
11.1 WALL SIGNAGE
11.2 INFORMATIONAL MATERIALS
11.3 VISITOR INTERACTION
11.4 TOURS AND DOCENTS
11.5 RECEPTIONS AND ARTIST TALKS
11.6 LECTURES AND FIELD TRIPS
11.7 CLASSES AND WORKSHOPS
11.8 DEVOTIONALS AND SERMONS

PROMOTION AND PUBLICITY
12.1 INTERNET PRESENCE
12.2 GALLERY CONTACT LISTS
12.3 NEWSLETTER
12.4 NEWS RELEASE
12.5 ANNOUNCEMENTS
12.6 ADS, INTERVIEWS, AND REVIEWS

USEFUL RESOURCES
13.1 CURATED EXHIBITS
13.2 ART EXHIBITION TUTORIALS
13.3 BOOKS
13.4 ORGANIZATIONS
13.5 ONLINE

SOURCE CREDITS

ACKNOWLEDGEMENTS

ABOUT THE AUTHORS

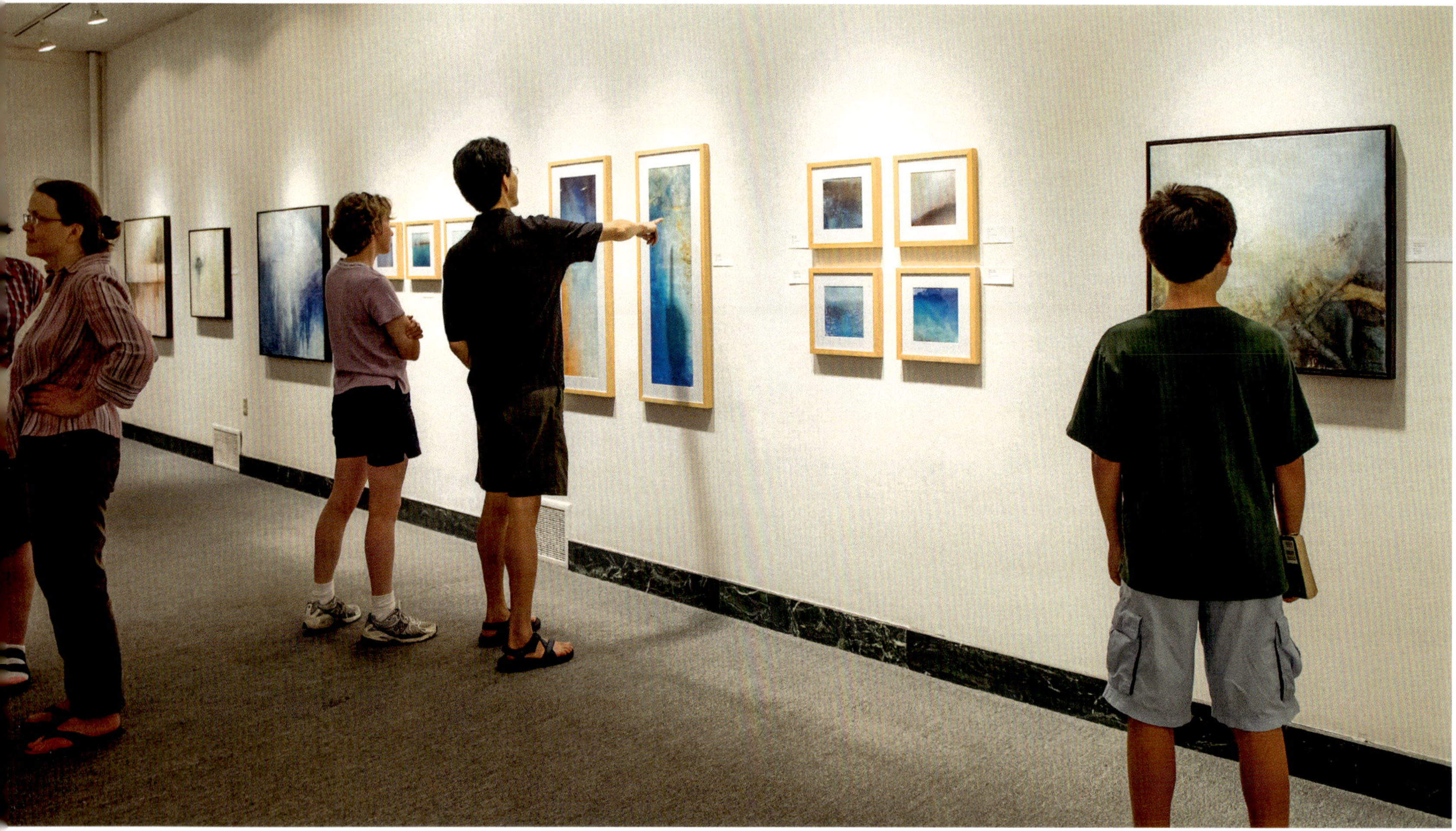

FOREWORD

W. DAVID O. TAYLOR

Stanley Hauerwas, the theologian and ethicist, once said that we do not see the world rightly just by opening our eyes. We see the world rightly, rather, by *training our eyes* to see the world rightly, which is another way of saying what C. S. Lewis observed: it is impossible to see the mystery, the beauty, or the terror of the world, fully at least, except by the help of others. As human creatures, our perception of the world is limited; as sinful creatures, our sight is broken so we need help to see the world as it truly is. This work of seeing rightly is, of course, God's work. All of us participate, but in a particular way, it is the work of visual artists.

In the beginning, God generates new life by speaking it into existence so that it might be beheld and enjoyed (Gen. 1:31). In the end, an epic spectacle marks the climax of history: "Behold, he is coming with the clouds, and every eye will see him" (Rev. 1:7). In Jesus' ministry, he heals the eyes of the blind and he blesses the eyes of those who perceive the work of God in their midst. While it is only by the work of the Holy Spirit that our eyes are fully healed, it is also true that God has staged a theater of his glory in creation, on display for all of humanity. Visual artists come along and say: *Look. Look carefully. Surrounding you is a world of beauty and of terror, fallen yet full of hope.*

Visual artists draw our attention to often-overlooked things, like the wonder of the color red or the curve of a bird's wing. They fix before us an image of a world broken by our own doing, but not abandoned by God. They make a plain room exceedingly lovely by the rich use of line and light. They combine absurd things to reveal the comical side of human life. In traditional or contemporary style, they invite us to notice the depth of creation, and the ways in which created things disclose the glory of God: lilies of the field, laundry, death, race, friendship, a well-made cup of coffee, or a chalice. Visual artists question our habits of sight, and they invite us to "pray with the eyes," to see the world as God sees it—our lives or neighbors or homes or churches or cities—and to be changed accordingly.

As you think about the possibility of visual art in the life of your church, and read through this handbook, I invite you to consider that our task together as church leaders and artists is not just the avoidance of false images. Nor is it just the removal of unfitting imagery in our church spaces. Our task instead is the provision of images and objects and structures which offer the physical eyes something good and true to look on, so that the eyes of our mind might be clarified and the eyes of our heart might be aroused for the sake of a deeper love of God and a more faithful engagement with a world that God so loves.

If this book equips your church in some way, deepens its worship, or enhances its mission, this Gallery Handbook will have fulfilled the purpose for which it was made. And that, on behalf of all in the CIVA community, will make us deeply happy.

SEEING THE UNSEEN

ROBERT COVOLO

If you are paging through this Handbook, it is likely that you are considering the launch of an art gallery in your church or seeking to further develop an existing one. In either case, congratulations! Launching or developing a church gallery can be a wonderful venture in the life of your congregation.

Because all galleries require a body of practical skills—lighting, framing, artist contracts, openings, and so on—this guide provides the kind of hands-on knowledge that will be important to your success. The pages of *Seeing the Unseen* aim to accomplish something more. In fact, there are as many kinds of church galleries as there are churches. Because of this, launching a gallery calls for something beyond well-executed "how-to" steps: it is an invitation to embark on an exciting and creative journey of faith!

Before starting on this journey, however, having clarity of purpose is essential. Why, for instance, should a church consider establishing a gallery? How might establishing an art gallery fit the church's calling? Are there theological reasons for establishing a gallery? To address these questions we begin with the book of beginnings: Genesis.

Our Creative Calling

The book of Genesis opens with God at work. Starting from an amorphous and murky soup (1:2), God methodically brings something new into existence. In the first three days of creation God produced a series of divisions: light/darkness, heaven/earth, sea/land. Having created the structures necessary for life, God then took three more days to fill the world with an amazing profusion of life—furnishing the heavens with all kinds of fowl, making the sea teem with aquatic creatures, and stocking the land with a host of diverse animals. Finally, capping off his masterful work, God makes humanity: "So God created man in his own image, in the image of God he created him; male and female he created them" (1:27).

What does it mean to be made in God's image? Although this question has received much speculation over the centuries, important clues are found in the preceding verses. In Genesis 1:2–26, we see God imposing order where order is lacking, filling what is empty, creating something arresting out of something crude. According to these verses, humanity was created to reflect God in his work, making something new, filling the world with good things, bringing design and purpose into formless disorder (2:7). Indeed, one detects this calling in God's charge to Adam and Eve: "And God blessed them. And God said to them, 'Be fruitful and multiply and fill the earth and subdue it . . . .'" (1:28).

In answer to God's forming and filling, human beings are to reflect their creator as they fill and form ("subdue") the world. In doing so they imitate God, creating things of value and beauty that were not there before. And so from the beginning of time to the present—from cave paintings to rocket ships—our race has been forming and filling the world with all kinds of things.

In his book *Culture Making*, Andy Crouch makes a surprising claim about the relationship of the artist to this God-given vocation to bring something new into the world. He states, "Something is added in every act of making. This is clearest in the realm of art, where the raw materials of pigment and canvas become more than you ever could have predicted."[1] While any number of cultural pursuits demonstrate this culture making impulse (surgery, plumbing, or farming), Crouch suggests a special resonance between the God who makes a *world* out of a primordial murky mass, and the capacity of artists who take raw and mundane elements such as paint, ink, or clay and through them create elaborate, imaginative worlds. It was this resonance between the work of the artist and God's creative activity that led theologian Abraham Kuyper to declare, "art must find its origin in our creation according to God's image."[2]

To be an image bearer is to be a culture maker. Within a biblical framework, therefore, culture making is not an accident of history but, rather, something first modeled by God. But as the story of the Bible unfolds and sin enters God's good creation (Gen. 3), this culture making impulse takes two paths. Some create culture according to the line of Cain: building cities filled with violence (Gen. 4:17–24) and towers out of prideful independence (Gen. 11:4). In response, God establishes another path. Beginning with the line of Seth and following through Noah, Abraham, and Jesus (Luke 3:23–38), God establishes a people who make culture for his glory. The Bible records that artists are included among such God-honoring culture makers: choreographers (Exod. 15:20), sculptors (25:9–40), silversmiths (31:1–11), songwriters (Pss.), composers (2 Chron. 5:11–14), storytellers (Judg. 9:7–20), and various other artisans (1 Kings 7:13–22).

As the people of God, the church continues this God-given calling to make culture to his glory. There are many ways we can do this. We can build schools and establish clinics, we can hold seminars on business ethics and child rearing. These are all good ways to reflect our God-given callings. Yet because there is something unique about the capacity of art for reflecting our world-making God, one of the great benefits of starting an art gallery is that it serves as a conspicuous rallying point for the local church as she seeks to align with her cultural commission. In other words, art galleries hold a distinct promise for reorienting and reinforcing the church's calling that was established at creation—a calling to be a God-honoring culture making people. This leads us to another reason for establishing a church gallery.

Faith in the Visual Register

Who hasn't been mesmerized by the infinite horizon of the sea, fog creeping into a canyon, snow-capped mountains peaking through the clouds after a storm? Such captivating visions remind us that God delights in producing stunning displays. Indeed, Scripture is eager to credit God as the source of creation's visual delights. As the writer of Genesis reminds us, "The Lord God made all kinds of trees grow out of the ground—trees that were *pleasing to the eye* . . ." (2:9). Scripture goes on, arguing that these displays not only please, they also serve as a form of language. As the Psalmist claims,

The heavens declare the glory of God, and the sky above proclaims his handiwork. Day to day pours out speech, and night to night reveals knowledge (19:1-2).

For the Psalmist, creation's visual displays are an important source of knowledge—providing a unique form of communication. The power of visual language is also exemplified in God's detailed directions for the construction of the Tabernacle (Exod. 25-30). Everything—from the exact specifications of the shape and design of various furnishings to the detailed depiction of the ornate bejeweled garments for Israel's priests—was designed to offer a visually rich symbolic world capable of instilling a deeply imaginative knowledge to Israel's worshippers. The rich visual languages of creation and the Tabernacle remind us that God wants his people to know him not only by means of the ear, but also with the eye. In fact all the senses testify to God, even our taste (Ps. 34:8)! This suggests another reason why the visual arts are important. The visual arts provide an indispensable form of meaning in a register that—although capable of complementing verbal communication—is not reducible to words.

At this point, some may be wondering if we've left out an important detail in the biblical witness. After all, doesn't the second commandment state that we are not to make graven images (Exod. 20:4)? This passage raises questions about the visual representation of God and has generated considerable debate among Christians over the centuries. Often such concerns are well founded. Nevertheless, we must be careful not to read into this commandment something that is not there. To be precise, the second commandment is not a ban against the production of images, but rather a ban against making images that we worship. In fact, in the subsequent chapters of Exodus, God commands the Israelites to create pomegranates on the hem of Aaron's garment, seraphim on the ark, and so on. These images were to complement and contribute to worship of the one true God. What's more, it should be noted that this command implicitly assumes that the visual holds a unique power—one that inspires responses from the deepest reserves of the heart. God's concern in the second commandment is not to remove meaningful form, but rather to clear space for God's most powerful visual display: revealing himself in the face of Christ.

The issue of the proper visual representation of God aside, the witness of Scripture is that we were created as image-making and image-reading creatures. Because of the importance of the visual in our lives, the church should take this aspect of our humanity seriously. As Christian art historian Hans Rookmaaker once remarked, "We should remind ourselves that Christ did not come to make us Christians or to save our souls only, but that he came to redeem us in order that we might be human, in the full sense of that word."[3] For Rookmaaker, if the Gospel is about making us fully human, then the church must address our God-given register of visual knowing. This is where a gallery can be of great service to the church. A gallery in the local church takes up this aspect of our humanity, providing a way for the people of God to understand and acknowledge, along with the Psalmist, that God is at work not only through verbal proclamation, but in and through a visual register as well.

We've seen that God is a God of visual artistry. This is true in two senses: first, God demonstrates in creation a love for resplendent visual display. And second, God creates creatures with an aptitude for the arts, including gifting individuals with the skill to make sculptures, to decorate things, to paint and draw. But before human hands first manipulated the physical world to create meaningful form, art was already in the mind of our good creator who decided to gift such capacities to his image bearers. Given that art is a God-given gift, it follows that art's ultimate value does not reside in any particular service it can render (culture making, communicating, etc.). Rather—as gift—it is to be celebrated for its intrinsic value. Or, as Hans Rookmaaker famously said, "Art needs no justification."[4] Regardless of its "usefulness," art remains valid simply because it is a good gift from our creator.

Of course, art does enable numerous actions that would not be possible in its absence. As Christian philosopher Nicholas Wolterstorff states, "works of art equip us for action. And the range of actions for which they equip us is very nearly as broad as the range of human action itself."[5] So far we've identified two important actions a church-based gallery makes possible: first, it offers a conspicuous way for the church to identify and embrace her calling as culture makers. And, second, it provides a site for reclaiming the God-given visual register. But the arts open up a host of other possibilities. So before concluding, let's consider three additional fields of action a church-based gallery makes possible. We can think of the direction of these types of action in terms of *moving in, moving out,* and *moving up.*

Moving In, Out, and Up
Moving In: This first set of actions that a church gallery makes possible can be understood in terms of empowering artists within a congregation. Historically the church celebrated a rich patronage of the arts. Yet, strangely, today many artists in the local church feel like they must justify their vocation. This situation is all the more troubling when one considers the demands of being an artist. These difficulties are compounded for Christian artists when they sense their church does not consider art a legitimate calling; or worse, they are viewed as dangerous to the health of the church. By establishing a gallery, the church makes it clear that artists are welcome and their calling is valued. Even more, it provides a rallying point for artists within the church community, offering a clear venue for Christian artists to collaborate as artists. Indeed, given the critical role that artistic collectives play in the larger art world today, such collaboration should be viewed as important for the future of Christian art.

Moving Out: Additionally, church-based galleries not only empower artists within the church, they also provide unique opportunities for the local church to serve the broader community. Calvin Seerveld once remarked, "The Lord God put art, this vessel of comfort and joy, into our hands..."[6] If indeed we are called to love and serve our neighbor, one wonders: how might the church use this vessel to bless others? This is an especially important question in light of the expanding role of the arts in our culture. It appears that increasing numbers of people are attempting to counter the drudgery of daily life with art's gift of color, line, shape, and form. Like a cup of cold water, a church-based gallery available to the larger public can serve to replenish those parched by the humdrum of life—offering a refreshing balm to heal tired imaginations.

But what about artists outside the church? Should a church-based gallery display the work of artists who do not regard themselves Christians or, for that matter, even religious? While it is impossible to fully explore this question here, there are reasons a church might consider inviting these artists to display their art. John Calvin noted that God gives artistic gifts not only to believers, but also to those outside the church.[7] Theologians have referred to such gifts as "common grace": God enabling those outside the community of faith to bless humanity and promote human flourishing. And because of such common grace, Christians should celebrate and enjoy excellent art, no matter who produced it. If indeed God has given his good gifts to artists outside the church, the body of Christ might consider inviting some of these artists to display their work. Of course, such an event should not be taken on without due consideration. Careful thought should be given to the proximity and function of such exhibits in relation to the worship of the church. Additionally, one must recognize that a church-based gallery is not a neutral space. As with showing a non-Christian film or reading a non-Christian author, considerations must be given regarding the time and place for the church to interact with such contributions. These are only two considerations and, undoubtedly, there are others. But such due diligence notwithstanding, exhibits featuring non-Christian art can serve as a valuable bridge between the church and the larger (artistic) community.

Moving Up: Finally, it is not only artists within the congregation and the larger community that will benefit from a church-based gallery: such a gallery stands to transform the church's worship as well. While Christians are familiar with worship employing the ear—voices joined in song, a well-crafted sermon, reciting a creed—a gallery within the local church provides an important place for the congregation to develop their appreciation for the visual register. Additionally, as visual artists feel embraced and empowered, some will desire to bring their gifts to assist with the worship of the church: seeking to complement the audibly rich worship space with visually poignant forms and symbols. Starting a gallery will stimulate fresh thinking and opportunities for the church's devotion and invite new questions, avenues, and participants with respect to the visual elements of the church's worship.

Before concluding, I offer this encouragement. A number of years ago, while serving as a pastor, a small group of visual artists from our church felt called to start a gallery. A curator was chosen, artists rallied, and a gallery was launched. It is beyond the scope of this introduction to detail all of the lives that were touched. But suffice it to say, what I have sketched out in this essay proved true. The gallery helped our church body identify and embrace her calling as culture making people; it provided a site for reclaiming a God-given visual register; it mobilized and empowered a community of artists within our church; it served as a bridge that connected our church with the broader community; and it inspired more visually-rich worship.

May this volume assist and inspire new journeys of faith!

1. Andy Crouch, *Culture Making: Recovering Our Creative Calling* (Downers Grove, IL: InterVarsity Press, 2008), 23.
2. Abraham Kuyper, *Wisdom & Wonder: Common Grace in Science and Art* (Grand Rapids, MI: Christian's Library Press, 2011), 148.
3. Hans Rookmaaker, *Art Needs No Justification* (Vancouver, BC: Regent College Publishing, 2010), 24.
4. Ibid., 39-42.
5. Nicholas Wolterstorff, *Art in Action* (Grand Rapids, MI: Eerdmans, 1980), 39.
6. Calvin Seerveld, *Bearing Fresh Olive Leaves: Alternative Steps in Understanding Art* (Carlisle, UK: Piquant, 2000), 20.
7. John Calvin, *The Institutes of the Christian Religion*, ed. McNeill, trans. Battles (Louisville, KY: WJK, 2006), 275.

DEFINING THE GALLERY PROGRAM

DEFINING THE GALLERY PROGRAM

Displays of human creative expression enrich the life of a church. Many communities of faith have chosen to embrace the visual arts—painting, drawing, sculpture, digital media, photography, and textile art—in ways that celebrate and reflect belief in a Creator God. This often includes designating spaces for art exhibits where the congregation and community gather for contemplation, inspiration, and conversation.

The church art gallery can assume many forms—everything from the repurposed fellowship hall, to well-lit exhibition areas in the sanctuary, to an architect-designed facility accessible to the public. A look at successful church art galleries across the country reveals a common component: each took time to form a visual arts team and define the gallery's purpose and policies.

A mission statement, which answers the question "Why should the church have an art gallery?" is the source from which all plans will emerge. A set of realistic goals that connect displays of art to primary audiences will keep the gallery program focused. In addition, the visual arts team must think through what their church believes is the function of the gallery and how it will operate. These guidelines and policies can be reviewed and adjusted periodically, but having them in place is helpful when various and sometimes difficult options present themselves.

1.1 VISUAL ARTS COMMITTEE

A passion for the visual arts shared by a few individuals in the church is often the catalyst for starting a gallery. The long-term success depends on the strength of an arts team or advisory committee to distribute responsibilities, build a base of expertise, and invigorate the planning process. A pastor's support and endorsement is necessary to integrate art displays into

SEEING THE UNSEEN

SECTION 1

the church's overall teaching program and ministry areas. Collaboration helps to grow everyone's appreciation for the arts and encourages the congregation to assume ownership of the gallery.

Within most churches there are people—representing a range of ages and backgrounds—who could be a great help in establishing and running a gallery. These include artists, art teachers, collectors, carpenters, administrators, graphic designers, architects, interior designers, writers, and people with marketing experience. Facilities and maintenance staff are a valuable resource for problem solving and advice about installation materials and methods.

The committee chairperson should be a visionary who is able to inspire enthusiasm for the program, motivate others to work together, oversee meetings and their agendas, and keep the operation on schedule and within budget. Over time and depending on the size of the program, it may become difficult to maintain a volunteer director to oversee the art gallery, at which point the church should decide to move the role into a paid position.

In some churches, gallery management is assigned to an arts pastor or staff member of the worship department. A director of visual arts ministry usually has responsibility for several programs besides the gallery. Institutions committed to high-quality exhibits that are intended to engage with the community outside of the church may retain the services of a professional curator or art consultant.

The visual arts committee needs to:

- Define the gallery mission and goals.
- Make and carry out policies.
- Plan the exhibition themes and dates.
- Oversee the selection of art.
- Establish and manage the budget.
- Coordinate art installations and supporting programs.

Specific duties can be shared among the team, considering each person's abilities and areas of expertise. It is a good idea to rotate gallery jobs so no one gets burned out and several people are able to take over in someone's absence. Ongoing areas of responsibility typically involve:

- Scheduling with the church calendar and staff.
- Communication with artists or the exhibit source.
- Art installation.
- Signage and interpretive materials.
- Publicity and promotion.
- Organizing openings/gallery functions.
- Fundraising.

The visual arts committee may want to consider giving a name to the gallery, which enhances the identity of the space and its program. In some churches, the gallery is named after the room it occupies, such as Fellowship Gallery, while others connect the gallery with the church's name, Gallery at All Saints, for example. There are also names drawn from a word associated with art, like Visions Gallery. The selection of a name could reference the gallery's mission, a donor who has funded the program, a religious figure, or the gallery's location.

Along with the name, a logo design will establish a visual identity for the gallery. This logo can be used on signage at the exhibition entrance, gallery stationery and forms, website and publicity materials.

1.2 MISSION STATEMENT

Knowing the gallery's audience is essential for shaping the mission. Most churches want a gallery that is mainly for the congregation's enjoyment and the spiritual growth of both adults and children. Others seek to have an outreach to the larger community and its artists. Some institutions may have the vision and resources to be a contributing presence in the cultural scene.

Once the intended audience is defined, the visual arts committee can determine a focus for the art that it will exhibit. Will the gallery have only sacred art, or a combination of religious work and art drawn from the congregation? Will artists from outside the church be invited to submit art? Are all kinds of art welcome in the gallery? Is the gallery space and budget appropriate for exhibiting culturally significant artworks that will interest the public? These are questions that need to be discussed and wrestled with in the process of shaping the new gallery.

A concise mission statement for the gallery that explains its "reason to be" and reflects a theology or philosophy of art and worship will be useful for guiding decisions about

> DIVERSIFY THE TYPE OF WORK THAT IS DISPLAYED. CHALLENGE THE NOTION OF WHAT ART IS AND WHAT IT CAN DO.
>
> — *Joyce Grimm*
> Creative Programs Consultant for Manresa Gallery at St. Ignatius Church, San Francisco, California

programming priorities. It should be short enough for people to remember and recite in a conversation and clear enough to be read and understood quickly on websites and in promotional materials. The best advice for creating a mission statement is to think of it as an introduction of the gallery to people who have no idea why it exists and what it displays, expressed in a way that indicates the core values that are important to the church and any strengths that differentiate this exhibition space from others.

Three sentences are all that is needed to craft a great mission statement:

- Describe what the gallery does.
- Describe how you do it, incorporating one or more of your values or strengths.
- Say why you do it.

After drafting these three sentences, delete, edit and rephrase the words, eliminating fuzzy ideas or jargon, until a memorable and articulate statement emerges. More than a slogan, it will succinctly explain the gallery's purpose and value. A longer mission statement that includes goals and a vision for future outcomes may be used internally. The most effective communication tool, however, is brief and simple. Examples of effective mission statements:

We want to cultivate and celebrate good creative work that honors God, serves people, and restores creation.
—Sojourn Arts and Culture,
Sojourn Community Church,
Louisville, Kentucky

Manresa Gallery presents traditional and contemporary art to highlight diverse expressions of faith. It provides a space for local and international artists to contemplate and expand spiritual practices through artistic expression and community dialogue.
—St. Ignatius Church,
San Francisco, California

The contributions of the artists in our community help us express and understand things about God that might otherwise be inexpressible. Our hope is that through these creative gifts, people will be directed toward the ultimate Creator—God Himself.
—All Angels' Church,
New York, New York

1.3 GALLERY GOALS

The following statements were drawn from a variety of church galleries and each represents a starting point from which a committee can think creatively about its goals. No two galleries will have the same intent, so discover together what best defines yours. These statements are organized by the relationship of an art gallery to worship, faith, artists, and community.

Relationship to Worship
- Affirm that creativity is a gift of God to humanity.
- Unite prayer with art process, inspiring original artworks that glorifiy God, encourage believers, and reach seekers.
- Enrich worship by another avenue that deepens spiritual experience.
- Exemplify God's creative spirit that permeates the Church and inspires the arts.
- Exhibit art that reflects the liturgical calendar.
- Use visual art to help us see the gospel afresh and inspire us to live it.

Relationship to Faith
- Visually demonstrate the intrinsic relationship between art and faith.
- Affirm aesthetics as a valid expression of faith, truth, Christian stewardship, and an intentional means of pedagogy and ministry.
- Display visual expressions of faith that add to the congregation's spiritual growth.
- Explore how visual language expresses ideas and truths beyond the spheres of words or music.
- Aid contemplation and meditation.
- Illustrate and illuminate biblical narratives.

Relationship to the Artist
- Provide an opportunity for parishioners to share their creative expressions.
- Appreciate artists within the Christian community.
- Support artists and art lovers by designating space to show and enjoy art.
- Validate the unique contributions of visual artists who create images that are thoughtful responses to God and reflections of divine beauty.

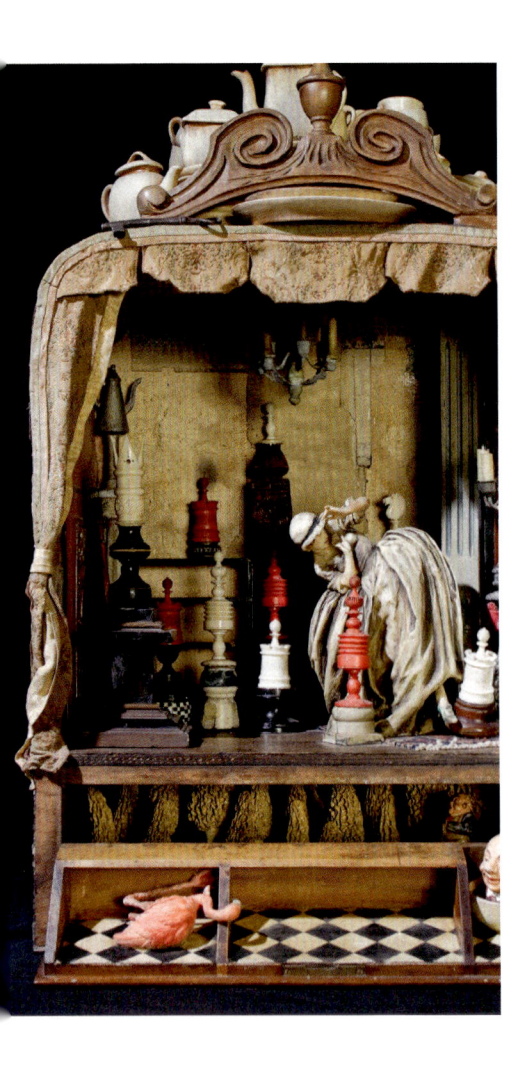

- Encourage artists to explore the significance of their art as an expression of faith.
- Create a bridge between an artistic vision and the viewer's spiritual reflection.

Relationship to the Community

- Provide an avenue for engaging with the neighborhood through the visual arts.
- Build relationships with other faith communities.
- Offer the local community a gallery of high quality sacred art.
- Be a respected presence in the local art community and civic life.
- Work with local schools to integrate the exhibits into art education curricula.
- Address social issues within the culture.

1.4 GALLERY POLICIES

It is advisable to set a few basic guidelines for the gallery's operation. These do not need to be unalterable, but gallery management will be easier if everyone knows the rules. For example:

- What department or church staff member has official oversight of the gallery?
- Will the art be insured while on display?
- Who has the final responsibility to accept or reject art that is submitted for exhibition?
- What is the process for handling requests to exhibit in the space?
- Is there a wait requirement before an artist can exhibit again in the gallery?
- Will the gallery give artists honoraria?
- Who is responsible for shipping costs?
- Will the gallery charge artists a fee?
- If art is available for sale, how are inquiries handled?
- Will prices be allowed in the show documentation or signage?
- Does the church expect to receive a commission or donation from sales?
- Is the gallery open to the public? If so, what days and hours will it be open?
- Will the gallery host artist receptions for the exhibits?
- Can food and drink be brought into the gallery space?
- Can visitors photograph the art in the gallery? Are flash photos permissible?
- Who has financial liability for damaged or stolen art?

2 GALLERY MODELS

GALLERY MODELS

In this section, three models are presented to illustrate how mission statement, goals, and policies will vary according to the gallery's purpose and audience. An art gallery cannot be everything to everyone. It must have a realistic focus to conserve resources and achieve good results. The hypothetical examples below highlight differences in things like art selection, programs, and budgets.

The first gallery model is designed primarily to benefit and edify the local congregation. The second envisions a gallery that will exhibit art for the congregation and the local faith community. The third model represents a professionally managed program that allows a church to actively engage in the cultural debate and contribute to the common good.

2.1 CONGREGATIONAL FOCUS

Mission
At Covenant Church, the displays of artistic expressions in the fellowship hall enrich our worship, support the education program, and bring people together for fellowship and conversation.

Goals
- Provide opportunities for parishioners, including our youth, to share their creative expressions.
- Display a wide variety of art media, subject matter, and themes.
- Promote through compelling images the church's mission and community service programs.
- Support the liturgical seasons and any special church-wide areas of study and discipleship.

Policies
- Exhibits will relate to issues of faith, biblical narrative, and life of the church.
- Gallery will accept artwork from amateur and professional artists within the local Christian community and may draw from the art collections of church members.
- There are eight shows per year, which open with a reception immediately after the Sunday morning service.
- The visual arts committee will work with the Worship Pastor to plan the year's exhibit schedule.
- The gallery is open an hour before and after regularly scheduled services.
- No artwork may be offered for sale through the church exhibition.
- All artworks will be displayed with labels. An artist statement or curator's note will be posted on the wall.
- Exhibits are promoted through the church website, newsletter, and Sunday bulletin.
- Gallery team and/or the exhibiting artists will install the art.
- Church budget for gallery expenses is $500 annually.

2.2 FAITH COMMUNITY FOCUS

Mission
Trinity Church Gallery presents quality art, informed by Christian beliefs, to the congregation and the local community. Our exhibits are a catalyst for communication between God and believer, offering lamentation for the way things are, imparting a vision for the way things could be, and providing visual metaphors for living by faith.

Goals
- Offer educational programs that expand viewers' visual literacy and art appreciation.
- Welcome other churches and organizations to the gallery for meditation and enjoyment.
- Feature art that helps people see the scriptures in new ways and promotes spiritual formation.
- Use the emotional power of art to inspire compassion and action to help the hurting.

Policies

- Art is selected by the Minister of Arts and the visual arts committee through exhibit rentals, calls-for-art, and artists invitations.
- There will be six shows annually, each two months long.
- A lecture should accompany each show; artists receive a speaking honorarium.
- Gallery hours are 9am-4pm, Tuesday-Thursday, and Sunday mornings during services.
- Gallery will not handle sales transactions, but may connect artist and buyer.
- Church will provide insurance of $40,000 for an exhibition.
- Show guides will be available for visitors to take home.
- Information panels describing the curatorial theme will be prepared for each show.
- Exhibits are promoted through the church's website, gallery contact list, postcards, and community event calendars.
- Art may only be installed by gallery-approved preparators.
- Church budget for gallery expenses is $3,000 annually. Donations to the church may be designated for the gallery program.

2.3 PUBLIC FOCUS

Mission

Third Millennium Gallery is located in the heart of downtown. The gallery, which is sponsored by St. James Church, exhibits contemporary artworks by national and international artists that provide a new lens for reflecting on religious faith and the sacred.

Goals

- Feature art that is creative, authentic, and relevant to contemporary culture.
- Create programs for the congregation and general public that educate, challenge, and inspire conversations about art, grace, and the human spirit.
- Collaborate with other art institutions of the city to host cultural events.

Policies

- Visual Arts Director is responsible for art curation, programming, and fundraising.
- There will be four shows annually, each three months long.
- Gallery will be staffed during open hours, 10am–5pm Tuesday–Saturday, and during the First Friday Night city art walk.

OUR CONGREGATION LOVES HAVING AN ART GALLERY IN THE CHURCH BUILDING. IT OPENS THEIR EYES TO HOW GOD CAN BE GLORIFIED. THEY ARE PROUD TO BE PART OF A COMMUNITY THAT EMBRACES THE CREATIVE ARTS.

—*Mary Ellen Johnson*
Director Traditional Music and Fine Arts for Austin Oaks Church, Austin, Texas

- Related programming for exhibits may include lectures, musical performances, and interactive art activities.
- Gallery follows current museum standards for exhibit signage and interpretation.
- Catalogs are produced for each exhibit.
- Art is insured for full value during shipping and while installed in the gallery.
- The gallery does not handle art sales, nor will it broker an artist-buyer connection.
- Professional art handlers will be retained for installing and shipping exhibits.
- Exhibits will be promoted through gallery and church websites, social media, news releases, and local newspapers.
- The gallery, as a 501(c)3 nonprofit, will operate independent of the church budget. The director submits an annual financial plan for the board's approval.

3

DESIGNING THE GALLERY SPACE

DESIGNING THE GALLERY SPACE

Selecting a welcoming place in a strategic location is essential for attracting visitors to the gallery. Its design affects how people perceive the art and navigate through exhibits. Subtle elements of aesthetics, lighting, and ambiance invite the viewer to draw close and linger. With creativity and imagination many churches have transformed unlikely spaces into stunning galleries.

Space for an art gallery can be found in a variety of places within church campuses, such as the main sanctuary, foyer, side chapel, wide hallway, classroom, or visitors center. Each of these arrangements has advantages and challenges. For example, a main passageway has great visibility, but less security. A gallery in a fellowship or dining hall is accessible, but may have difficulty exhibiting three-dimensional objects. Installing art inside the worship area poses problems for visitors when the sanctuary is in use. A dedicated art exhibition room can accommodate a wide variety of objects, but may attract less traffic than other spaces.

Wilshire Baptist Church in Dallas, Texas, installs temporary art exhibits throughout the building, matching each show with an appropriate space. A series of big, bold paintings could be hung in the lobby and a small exhibit of intimate works in an alcove. *Seeing Christ in the Darkness*, a Bowden Collections exhibit of works by Georges Rouault, was installed during Lent in a quiet room next to the worship area with subdued lighting that encouraged reflection and meditation.

Location influences the gallery's overall purpose. An exhibit buried deep within the church complex does not lend itself to community outreach. In contrast, a gallery situated near an entrance, such as Fourth Presbyterian Church's Loggia Gallery in downtown Chicago, can more easily invite the public inside. The Gallery at Saint Christopher's Church in Chatham, Massachusetts, has thousands of visitors annually because it is located street-side in a popular downtown shopping area.

In reality, the existing church facility determines the space that can be used for art displays;

and the space determines the kind of art exhibits that can be installed. When a church building is being constructed or remodeled, more specific planning enables the church to have an optimum gallery for safely displaying a range of artworks accessible to the congregation and community.

Even without dedicated gallery space, a church can have an art exhibition program. Some groups are experimenting with off-campus galleries located within the town's art center or another building separate from the church. These could be rented retail space, a lobby provided by a local business, and collaboration with an art center or school.

3.1 WALLS, PARTITIONS, AND PANELS

False walls can be built over existing elements to achieve a unifying space and to allow art to be hung where there are unsuitable surfaces or architectural features. Movable partitions that can be carried into place, constructed on wheels, or suspended from the ceiling with cables create rooms within a room and provide flexibility to customize the space for each show. Adjustable walls are excellent for managing traffic flow, highlighting special art pieces, and increasing the number of works that can be accommodated in the exhibition.

There may be knowledgeable carpenters on the exhibitions team or church staff who could design and construct temporary walls for the gallery. Compare the cost of hiring a local contractor with purchasing modular wall systems and partitions from specialist vendors, such as Armstrong and MBA Design and Display Products.

A set of lightweight, portable display panels are an option for occasional exhibits of small artwork. These interlocking systems can be set up in minutes and are typically used in art fairs and exhibition booths. Popular vendors, such as Pro Panels and Screenflex, can be located through an Internet search for "art display panels." The panels are typically covered in black, gray, or buff carpet and most companies offer several sizes, hanging hardware, matching pedestals, and construction options.

One church rents portable panels from a local art club to set up a display of religious-themed art on the church's front patio during the city's annual street art fair. While it was meeting in a school gymnasium awaiting the completion of its new building, Open Door Church in San Mateo, California, created a charming "pop up" gallery every Sunday morning with these display units.

With any wall, it is important to know the weight that it can safely hold. Conditions such as thickness of the drywall, spacing of wall studs, and if there is backer-board may affect the load a wall can bear, and therefore determine the limits and parameters of the kind of art the gallery can exhibit. When designing and constructing the gallery space, follow the manufacturer-specified weight range and the advice of experienced builders.

3.2 HANGING SYSTEMS

Every gallery has to decide how the art will be hung on its walls. Budget, wall construction, and aesthetics combine to affect the ultimate decision. There are three main ways to hang art: hanger/nail/screw; track/hanger/hook; picture molding/monofilament/D-ring.

The first and traditional approach is to use picture hangers nailed into the wall or roundhead screws inserted part way into the vertical surface. This system is elegant, inexpensive, flexible, and can accommodate nearly any kind of art. There is very little restriction as to where the art can be mounted. The downside is that the walls have to be repaired and repainted after every exhibition. It also demands precise measuring and many tools. This hanging method would not work for walls that can't securely hold a nail or screw, such as stone, adobe, or concrete.

With the track and hanger option, an aluminum track or rail is attached horizontally to either the wall or ceiling. Vertical hangers —typically metal rods or nylon cables and cords—are placed anywhere along the span of track, and hooks attach the art to the hangers. Although ceiling-mounted tracks support less weight than the wall-mounted, they are a good solution for walls that are made of vintage wood, marble, brick or have special finishes that would be irreparably damaged by nail holes. The hooks and fittings used to suspend artwork from the hangers offer different options for weight loads and security.

MANY ARTISTS IN THE CHURCH WOULD DEARLY LOVE TO SHOW THEIR ART; TO KNOW THEIR CALLING IS VALUED AND USEFUL FOR MINISTRY.

—*Mark Wingfield*
Associate Pastor for Wilshire Baptist Church, Dallas, Texas

This kind of system allows the art to be easily centered and hung quickly. It also eliminates the need to repair and paint the walls. On the negative side, the track method is inadequate for large or heavy art, the rods or cables are visible, and the system can be an expensive investment for some gallery budgets.

There are many companies that sell art hanging systems, such as Absolute, Arakawa, AS Hanging Systems, Gallery System, STAS, Systematic Art and Walker Display. Each offers a range of options and prices.

The molding and monofilament hanging method dates from the late nineteenth century and was popular into the Art Deco era. Classic ogee picture rail molding, available at most lumber stores, is installed at about 7.5 feet from the floor. Monofilament (fishing line) is strung through D-rings or eye screws on the back of the art and over a flat S-hook or tapered picture rail hook that is hung on the molding. Advantages of this system: no wall damage, centering the art vertically and horizontally is fairly easy, and the monofilament is almost invisible. The disadvantage is that installing the art requires a ladder, two people, and if the art does not have D-rings attached near the frame's top, it will tilt out from the wall.

3.3 LIGHTING FIXTURES AND WINDOWS

Lighting is of great importance for viewers' full appreciation of the art. On one hand, everyone has been in a gallery where the illumination is so poor that it is nearly impossible to view the exhibit or read the labels. On the other, if the lighting is too strong, the art and background areas fight each other for attention. Investing in a good lighting system is probably the most important expenditure that a church can make for an exhibition space.

As challenging as good lighting can be for a church gallery, direct sunlight can pose considerable problems, because ultraviolet (UV) light will cause fading or other damage to artwork. This is particularly true for works on paper and textile art. Either eliminate hanging objects on walls that are exposed to direct sunlight, or find a way to shade the light entering the room. Window film is available that can block up to 99 percent of UV rays and solve problems with heat and glare without blocking the view. Special UV light filters and guards can be put over fluorescent lamps to eliminate their harmful radiation.

As a general rule, the best illumination for displaying art is a combination of diffuse (room/ambient) and directional (exhibit) lighting. The goal is to light the art work at a brighter level than the room. Most galleries prefer to use track lighting that permits the light to be specifically directed and adjusted for each exhibition. Adjustable track lights provide flexibility for illuminating art of varying sizes and placement within the display space. Some light canisters with variable beam angles can adjust to 15, 30, 45, and 60 degrees. Track lights should be far enough away from the wall to avoid hot spots inside dark areas. Install the track so that the distance from the display is about a third of the height of the wall. Do not use lights that clip onto a painting's frame. Not only do these look unprofessional, but they can cause heat damage to the artwork.

The most common types of light bulbs used for illuminating art objects are incandescent, halogen, compact fluorescent, and LEDs. Each offers advantages and disadvantages in terms of cost, color rendering, heat generation, energy efficiency, and life span. Fluorescent lights and LED bulbs are currently not the best for illuminating artwork because they tend to alter an object's color. Better choices are a combination of halogen and incandescent lights that meet energy efficiency guidelines. New fiber-optic products that generate low heat, no UV and no infrared rays are available for exhibits of light sensitive art materials.

SEEING THE UNSEEN

SECTION 3

If the church gallery has picture windows that look onto a street or public sidewalk, have a plan for lighting the exhibit at night. Installing a two-circuit track system, with one track on a timer, allows a few selected lights to illuminate the gallery even when the church is closed.

3.4 STORAGE

A behind-the-scenes storage area is useful for holding art installation equipment and supplies for gallery receptions. The room will need some shelving to keep light bulbs, tools and to store smaller works of art. The space should be large enough to hold pedestals, ladders, and the boxes and crates in which the art has been delivered.

When the show is not hung on the gallery walls, it should be stored in a locked room or closet. Avoid storing art in a space that has another function, such as a maintenance closet or supply room where people are coming in and out and accidents could easily happen. When this kind of shared room is the only resort, use partitions to physically separate the artwork area and restrict access to it.

Put the art in a location that is not in airflow passage such as vents and windows. When dealing with highly valuable artwork, standard guidelines recommend maintaining the relative humidity of the storage room and gallery between 45–55 percent, and the temperature at a constant between 65–75 °F. Twenty-four hour air conditioning is the most effective way to protect fine art from serious fluctuations in humidity and temperature. If the room is near a flood source, such as water pipes or radiator, all art objects should be elevated several inches above the floor.

If exposed art will be sitting on the floor, cover the floor with carpeting, rubber mats, or cardboard. When the gallery must temporarily store framed works that are not in boxes or crates, it is best to wrap the art in plastic or a clear plastic bag to avoid scratching the frames and glazing (glass or acrylic). Some artwork, such as textiles and pieces with metallic finishes or special varnishes should be wrapped first in acid-free paper, fabric, or Tyvek if they will be encased in the plastic for more than a few weeks. Additional guidelines for how to properly store artworks are provided in *Section 9.2: Receiving, Storing, and Packing.*

FUNDING THE GALLERY 4

FUNDING THE GALLERY

The cost of funding a church gallery can range from very little to substantial, depending on the gallery's mission and focus. Once the space has been constructed and outfitted with lighting and a hanging system, the most basic program would only require photocopies, labels, and installation supplies. So expense need not be a deterrent to launching a visual arts ministry. Churches that rent exhibits, retain jurors, maintain insurance, develop promotional and interpretive materials, and host opening events will need larger budgets. Galleries committed to mounting culturally significant art shows will often require funds to cover artist stipends, guest curators, professional art installation, and shipping costs.

There are many excellent galleries supported by the valiant efforts of volunteers. Churches that consider the visual arts integral to their programs will have paid staff for the gallery's management.

Determining the costs that will be incurred over the course of the year and writing a budget will help the officers of the church understand the financial needs of the gallery. Major donors will also want to see the gallery budget. A budget can be outlined in a number of ways. One method is to estimate the costs associated with each show. Another would be to summarize individual items such as, labor, materials, publicity, honoraria, graphic design, and printing. Any anticipated income should be included in the budget. The following section describes a number of ways for funding a church art gallery.

4.1 CHURCH BUDGET ALLOWANCE

When the gallery is a valuable and vibrant part of congregational ministry, it should be a line item in the church's annual budget. It is the job of the visual arts committee to present a convincing argument to the church leaders for including the gallery in their financial planning.

Even if the church budget is insufficient to support an art gallery, a gallery fund can usually be set up to run through the church's bookkeeping system. This account should be able to take donations that are designated for this purpose, and allow checks to be written by the treasurer to reimburse expenses and pay bills. This is the best way to have a record of the money associated with the gallery, which eventually can be used to establish a budget allowance.

4.2 FRIENDS OF THE GALLERY

Establishing a Friends of the Gallery program has several benefits, one of which is the development of a group of people who love art and want the gallery program to thrive. They can become a volunteer force that helps with openings and invites people to events. If this group is organized with an annual membership fee and commitment to donate to the gallery fund, they can be a valuable source of financial support. Consider ways to encourage membership, such as private tours and an invitation to dinner with the artist.

4.3 SPONSORS AND DONORS

Sometimes it is possible to attract an individual, family, corporation, or organization to sponsor an exhibition. Think creatively about who would have an interest in a particular show. A local bookstore might want to contribute to a calligraphy display. An architectural firm may find it beneficial to underwrite an art exhibit that explores structural ideas. Involving art clubs, schools, and community groups could generate financial support. Even another department in the church may want to sponsor a show that relates to their area of ministry. Prepare an exhibition prospectus for the potential sponsor that describes the show, presents its benefits to the community, and states how much it will cost.

In-kind donations are another valuable resource. For example, a member of the church who is a caterer may offer to supply refreshments for the reception, or a graphics designer may create the exhibit poster and invitation cards. However, it is not wise to rely on the kindness of congregants for the long term. Contingency funds should be retained for when the service is a burden for the congregant.

Many churches, especially within older mainline denominations, have memorial funds that may be a source for the gallery program. A memorial fund is established to receive money that is given to the church to honor a deceased individual.

4.4 GRANTS

Another option for funding an exhibit and its associated programming is a grant from a private foundation. Grants for church art galleries are not easy to find or secure, but they are possible. For example, The Calvin Institute for Christian Worship has awarded grants for exhibits that relate to worship and benefit a community beyond the local congregation.

The 2015 website of the White House Office of Faith-Based and Neighborhood Partnerships links to grant opportunities and resources for projects that serve community needs.

Some churches have endowments to which the visual arts committee may submit a grant proposal. Family foundations, local community foundations, and denominational grants are other possibilities. In each case, the granting organization will have specific application qualifications. So it is important to research carefully before applying to determine if the grant requirements are a good match for the gallery's program.

GrantSpace.org,, an online service of the Foundation Center, provides easy-to-use, self-service tools to help non-profits become more viable grant applicants.

> IF THE VISION FOR AN ART GALLERY IS IN YOUR HEART, DON'T LET IT STAY A DREAM. MOVE FORWARD AND ADJUST AS YOU GO. THE ARTISTS WILL HELP YOU, BECAUSE THEY ARE GRATEFUL FOR THE OPPORTUNITY TO SHARE THEIR GIFTS.
>
> —*Dan Hammer*
> Worship, Music and Arts Director for John Knox Presbyterian Church, Seattle, Washington

4.5 AUCTIONS

An art auction can be a fun way to raise money, promote artists, and develop art collecting. Auctions can be held online or in a festive venue. A popular auction is to give artists an identical material or object for transformation by their unique artistry. The auction does not have to be limited to art. It can include a variety of services: web design, antiques, or a vacation home weekend. Tickets to the event may be sold if a dinner, music, or another form of entertainment is included.

A note about selling artist-donated artwork: the organization should carefully handle and display the art and try to get the highest price for it, perhaps by setting minimum bids and reserve prices. At the end of the auction, give the name and contact information of the buyer to the artist for her records. Artists who are frequently asked to donate to charity auctions prefer to support those that show respect for their contribution.

4.6 ARTIST COMMISSIONS AND FEES

A church gallery's purpose differs from a commercial gallery in that its main goal is educational, not financial. However, many churches make provisions for the sale of available art by referring the potential buyer to the artist. Some churches ask the artist to donate back to the gallery a percentage of a sale made through the gallery exhibit. This might vary from 10% to 30% of the sale price. There is no fixed rule related to sales and it is best to have a frank discussion early on in the establishment of the gallery.

When an art organization issues a call for entry to the art community (also known as call for art, call for artists, request for proposal, or prospectus), it is not uncommon for artists to pay a small fee for each submission. The fees, which typically cover the cost of the show or provide an honorarium for the juror, range from $10 to $20 per entry. An alternative option is to request a contribution from each participating artist to help defray advertising and reception costs. Although artist fees are commonplace in the secular art world, they can be inappropriate if the purpose of the church gallery is missional or liturgical. Some churches would not expect artists to fund its ministry either through fees or sales commissions.

4.7 COLLABORATIONS AND CROWD FUNDING

Exhibition costs can be shared between several churches if the artworks will tour to their respective galleries. For example, the participating churches could share the cost of an announcement postcard that contains information for each of the installations, and other expenses for curator services, artist stipends, signage, and show catalog.

Many artists and cultural producers are increasingly turning to funding sources that leverage new technologies and tap into Internet-based social networks. Crowd funding websites such as Indiegogo and Kickstarter allow individuals to pool their money and collectively finance creative projects and art nonprofits.

Another new idea is crowd patronage. Online platforms such as Patreon facilitate the ongoing funding of artistic productions by collecting small monthly contributions for individuals and organizations engaged in creative activity. Through an art subscription program, patrons who fund an exhibition receive something in return, such as an artist's print, a show catalog, or the privilege of attending a special reception with the artist.

BUSINESS ADMINISTRATION 5

BUSINESS ADMINISTRATION

Managing an art gallery, even a nonprofit one, involves administrative duties to ensure the safety of the work and to protect the interests of both the exhibitors and the church. In the spirit of professional cooperation with artists, the gallery will want to address issues of security, insurance, and loan agreements.

5.1 SECURITY

There is risk involved in having an art gallery that is open and accessible to the public and parishioners. It is best to think through all the implications of the location and make provisions to secure the work from theft, vandalism, and accidents. If the gallery is in a very public area or near an entrance, installing a security alarm or video surveillance system may be a consideration. A nearby reception desk may be sufficient to keep an eye on the exhibition. Assigning volunteers or student interns to watch the gallery during open hours is another precaution.

5.2 INSURANCE

At some point, the gallery must work out a policy regarding insurance and liability issues. Most established artists and art rental services will not participate in uninsured exhibits. The church's business office can obtain recommendations from its insurance company and legal counsel. Solutions will vary depending on criteria such as the type of insurance policy, kinds of shows, rental contracts, artist agreements, and unique security issues.

For example, a predetermined rider of $20,000 to $50,000 can be added to the church's general liability policy, which covers the artwork when it is in the custody of the gallery. If a particular exhibit will have a higher value, it can be worked out on a case-by-case basis. The insurance terms of some churches will cover art shows without a rider if the total value is under a certain amount. Art exhibit rental agreements typically require the church to insure the show while it is in transit. The gallery should be clear in its communications with artists shipping work, regarding who's responsible for the cost of insurance.

The insurance company will require a list of works in each exhibit, including artist's name, title, materials, size, and retail value. If the gallery has an insurance limit per object, the artist will be responsible for covering the value above that amount. When there is a claim, the artist must provide some proof of value, such as a sales receipt for a similar piece of work.

The law in some states may hold the sponsor of an exhibition responsible for damages to artwork whether or not the sponsor has insurance. If the gallery does not insure the artwork, it is advisable to require each participating artist to sign a liability waiver. If the gallery plans to use images of the artist's work for publicity purposes, such as postcard, poster, press release, or exhibit catalog, it may be necessary to get the artist's permission. The easiest way is to put these stipulations in the artist registration form or loan agreement. An example of wording:

I release [name of gallery], [name of church], and all others affiliated with [name of church] from liability due to loss or damage of my artwork. I understand that I am solely responsible to provide my own insurance for the art exhibition. In addition, I grant permission for [name of gallery] to reproduce an image of my art for publication in an exhibition catalog. I understand that my name will be used in connection with the art exhibition; and I agree that images of my art may be used for publicity including on the Internet.

5.3 ARTIST HONORARIA

When an artist is asked to prepare a lecture, travel, or create original art specifically for a church installation, it is customary to recognize and thank them by providing an honorarium to pay for the artist's costs. These stipends can range from $100 to several thousand dollars, depending on the artist's reputation, how far they must travel, the nature of the work, and preparation time. The honorarium is intended as a show of respect to the artist's professional qualifications. While the artist could work without any expectation of compensation, the congregation that is benefiting from the work can express their gratitude in a tangible way with this gift.

5.4 ARTIST LOAN AGREEMENT

A simple agreement that defines the respective responsibilities of the gallery and the artist fosters open communication and avoids misunderstandings. The basic one-page document is signed by the gallery representative and the artist, specifies the exhibition title, show dates, and space where the art will be installed. It will also state the amount of any stipend that is to be paid.

Example of responsibilities of the artist:

- Deliver ready-to-hang art by [date], with responsibility for shipping cost.
- Complete and sign a loan agreement.
- Provide an accurate list of the pieces with values and label information by [date].
- Provide information requested by gallery for education panels and publicity by [date].
- Incur no expenses on the gallery's behalf.
- Be available to present a program for the artist talk.
- Work with gallery staff to arrange the return of artwork at the close of the show.

Example of responsibilities of the gallery:

- Insure the artwork from the time the gallery takes possession until it is returned to the artist.
- Prepare loan agreement/condition reports.
- Prepare education panels and labels.
- Publicize the exhibit through newsletter, postcard, and press release.
- Provide the artist with 50 invitations to the opening reception.
- Unpack, install, and repack the artwork.
- Return artwork to the artist by [date], with responsibility for shipping cost.
- Give the artist contact information to visitors who have inquiries.

The loan agreement may provide more or fewer details than the above example. Some galleries include a clause alerting the artist that the church reserves the right to remove any work it deems inappropriate for the space.

> THROUGH THE GALLERY PROGRAM, OUR CHURCH MEMBERS DEVELOP VISUAL LITERACY. THEY CAN LOOK AT ART IN OTHER VENUES AND HAVE MEANINGFUL INSIGHTS AND ENJOYMENT.
>
> —*Ann Williams*
> Visual Arts Director for Lincoln Berean Church, Lincoln, Nebraska

6 PLANNING EXHIBITS

PLANNING EXHIBITS

Planning exhibits is the fun and creative part of running a church art gallery. Choosing a theme and thinking through the purpose of an exhibit are the elements that separate a mundane display of art from an event that engages visitors in meaningful interaction with ideas, imagination and emotions. A great exhibition is not only about the art, but also the experience that viewers internalize for a lifetime of reflection. The curator's primary concern is the audience and their interaction with the art.

Quality art presented in a professional atmosphere will have an impact on how the gallery is viewed internally and externally. Unfortunately, many churches have been content with mediocrity when it comes to their art shows. In today's image-saturated world, any church that wants to have a voice in the marketplace of ideas and contemporary culture must present works of authenticity, integrity, and exemplary craft.

This is not to say that amateurs are eliminated from participation. With creative thinking and a spirit of hospitality, the gallery can find ways for many to show their handiwork in a variety of media. Whether the audience focus is congregational or public, every exhibition should aspire to the highest standards possible in work and presentation.

Generally speaking, art shows are curated, invitational, juried, or open. A curated show means the art has been selected by a curator who has a unique vision or story to tell with the exhibition. An organizer asks specific artists to participate in an invitational exhibit. A juried show has an art expert or a panel of judges who choose works that have been submitted through a call for entry. An open or non-juried exhibit is inclusive and whatever is submitted will be displayed. A church gallery may decide to use any or all of these methods over time.

6.1 LENGTH AND FREQUENCY

Many commercial galleries change their shows monthly. Museums tend to have shows that run longer, even five or six months. These institutions have very different goals from each other that influence the length of time they want the art to be seen. The commercial gallery hopes to sell art and the museum's main purpose is to educate.

There is no recommended number of exhibits for a church gallery. When planning the frequency and length of shows, the committee will want to consider the time and energy it takes to secure and mount an exhibit. Fewer shows reduce the work involved over the course of a year. Longer shows allow the congregation to become deeply familiar with the art and develop a shared visual language.

Some churches prefer to exhibit art only during the Advent and Lenten seasons. Cross View Lutheran Church in Edina, Minnesota, has just one solo artist or thematic show a year that complements an annual juried exhibition. Some church galleries close during the summer months unless, of course, the church is located in a summer vacation area when a show is very important.

In planning the gallery exhibition calendar, the visual arts committee should avoid last minute rushes and leave time for cancellations. A typical church gallery will schedule its shows a year ahead, more for special exhibits and less for member participation shows.

6.2 CURATORIAL RESEARCH

The role of the curatorial team is to select, display, and interpret works of art so that visitors to the gallery are informed and inspired. It is part of their job to understand the current discourse in art and theology, have a working knowledge of contemporary art trends and become familiar with the local community of artists. To keep current, they can visit museums together, attend gallery openings, read art reviews, peruse artist websites, and occasionally meet with artists in their studios.

Some churches have members with formal training or experience in art history, studio art, or theology and the arts. Accessing the expertise of these professionals can add quality and depth to the gallery exhibits. If these resources are not available, it is important for the curator to spend time acquiring information that will help produce intellectually challenging, aesthetically pleasing, and culturally relevant art shows. This ongoing investigation will focus on particular themes, narratives, and art genres according to the gallery's exhibition plans.

There has never been an easier time for the layperson to acquire information about the intersection of image and spirit and to identify artists whose practices embrace the spiritual. Today an abundance of excellent books, blogs, podcasts, conferences, and websites dedicated to the Christian art movement are available. There are organizations that provide dynamic networks of people who are interested in integrating visual art into church communities of many denominations and worship traditions.

In most major metro areas, there are usually a number of churches with visual arts programs. Interesting things can happen if the different gallery directors and arts ministers share information and encouragement. Arts of the Covenant—a group of visual artists who live in the San Francisco Bay Area—meets monthly, posts news on a website, and produces religious-themed exhibits that tour different churches in the region. Local church gallery directors use the group as a resource for art and artists.

6.3 THEMES AND MESSAGES

Every church will have a different process for selecting exhibition themes. It could be the responsibility of one person, such as the visual arts committee chair, or a curator working with an advisory team under a pastor's oversight. There is no one correct approach. The process eventually should end with one sentence that defines the theme and sets the tone and scope of the exhibit. All the show's parts—from the art to interpretive labels—will be driven by this "big idea." It is the single communication objective that guides the team to focus the purpose of the show, such as a cross cultural exchange, interfaith dialogue, exploration of a topic, celebration of a religious season. With a cohesive exhibit plan, as visitors leave the exhibit they will have thoroughly understood what it was about and found it personally meaningful.

The "big idea" can be expanded into a short curatorial statement to help viewers understand the relationship of the art to the theme and make them curious about the work. A typical statement will be about 150–250 words. It establishes the premise of the show, mentions the range of artistic approaches, and suggests the wider significance of the theme. The statement should be written with thoughtful consideration of the audience. If the show's purpose is to engage the general public, avoid church-speak, and if most of the viewers will be believers who are unfamiliar with art, avoid art-world jargon. Take care to define any terms that are essential to the theme of the exhibition. The statement can be provided in a handout or printed on a wall poster.

If the church gallery is exploring a biblical story or spiritual theme, the curator will want to examine the issues and read relevant scriptures before selecting the art. A pastor's oversight and guidance can be most helpful in this area, especially for identifying artwork that is more conceptual than illustrative. Enrolling in a class or studying a book with other like-minded people could help a curator understand an exhibition narrative in the context of art history.

Tandem with issuing the call for entry, some curators will sponsor a lecture for local artists as a catalyst for new art work that fits the theme. For example, if a show is planned about "patterns in nature," a botanist or mathematician could give a talk about fractals. For an exhibit of art that illuminates hymns, the music director could present the history of cantorial music and congregational song. A theologian might explore biblical metaphors for redemption to inspire an exhibit of art made with found objects and repurposed materials.

6.4 CONTROVERSY

Sometimes a visitor may not agree with the value or appropriateness of a particular artwork in the church art gallery. An entire exhibit could be perceived negatively, taking the curatorial team by surprise. Negative reactions may originate from aesthetic, emotional, theological, and religious reasons. "Offensive" is a relative word. It is often the result of viewers' individual experiences, disagreement with an agenda that someone thinks is being promoted by the exhibit, and differences in art appreciation and knowledge.

Controversy may come up during the planning or marketing phases, at any time after the exhibition opens, and continue after it closes. As controversy escalates, some people will express opposition to an offending artwork even if they have not seen it.

Almost every gallery has a story to tell. One gallery director caused a flap by showing Orthodox iconography in an Evangelical venue. Another director was compelled to remove an artwork with difficult subject matter that disturbed a congregant. An exhibition of art quilts was rejected by a young worship team that deemed the genre unsuitable for their contemporary service. A pastor recalled how one large painting of a nude crucifixion offended half the congregation. The other half was angry that anyone could possibly be offended.

Good art is inherently provocative in part because it communicates ideas and new perspectives that spark emotions and discourse. Which is exactly why visual art should have a place in churches and religious institutions. Sensitivity to congregants' concerns and clarification of the gallery's role are important for avoiding controversy that could impact the gallery's viability or erode goodwill and the community's trust. Artists, curators, and gallery directors, however, cede their creativity and responsibility if their response to controversy is self-censure and reluctance to show art that is a catalyst for discourse, enlightenment, and serious social engagement.

The curator or director of a church-based gallery must determine with every show how the artwork is potentially redeeming. In this regard, the gallery's mission statement is critical. The images displayed in the gallery should fit the mission of the gallery. For example, if the gallery exists primarily as a showcase for church members' creative expressions, complaints regarding quality and content can be measured against the goals of inclusiveness and fellowship. Artwork that makes viewers uncomfortable can be justified if it is aligned with a gallery's goal to affirm aesthetics as a valid expression of truth. Abstract and edgy contemporary art will be included in a gallery that seeks to educate and expand congregants' visual literacy.

If censorship is inevitable, the gallery may specify in the artist agreement that it maintains the right to exhibit a work or not. Clarity on this issue gives artists the option to withdraw from the exhibit if censorship is a problem for them.

A well-crafted show statement, good signage, informed gallery sitters, and an artist talk are helpful to address questions about why certain pieces may be on exhibition. The gallery mentioned above dealt constructively with concerns by inviting leaders from the local Orthodox Christian community to speak about the history and meaning of icons. Instead of a default to close the show, the gallery became a catalyst for interfaith interaction and a learning opportunity. Having a team responsible for choices is also helpful, so no one individual is faulted. Counsel from an advisory panel early in the exhibit planning process can inform the presentation, interpretive labels, and programs.

When controversy arises, communication is crucial:

- Designate a spokesperson to answer questions and address concerns.
- Keep the focus on the art, artist, or topic.
- Avoid taking the comments personally.
- Acknowledge different points of view and alternative meanings.
- Put the show in the context of the gallery's mission and exhibition history.
- Explain the curatorial selection process.
- Have a feedback method for viewers to express their thoughts.
- Provide opportunities for community discussion and meaningful dialogue.
- Consider possible solutions, such as relocating the offending artwork.
- Maintain a spirit of grace and peace.

7 KINDS OF EXHIBITS

KINDS OF EXHIBITS

The gallery's goals will determine the exhibits that grace its walls. A church that has decided to show only sacred art can pass over other kinds of creative expressions. If non-sacred options are open to the committee, then a wider range of shows may be considered. Within the stated mission, it is important to organize a cycle of shows that appeal to various ages, honor different levels of knowledge, respect a diversity of cultural backgrounds, and introduce viewers to a range of media and techniques.

The most obvious source of art is local artists, both in the church and in the community. In any geographic area there are usually dozens of good artists and craftspeople from which to choose. Part of the scouting includes contacting art groups and schools to get names, and attending local shows to see what is in the region.

If there are other nearby churches that have galleries, it might work well to exchange exhibits, arranging for the art to be transported to the next venue immediately after the last one closes. Sharing conserves curatorial efforts and expands the galleries' possibilities. Artists will appreciate the increased visibility.

Many older churches have assembled collections of fine art through artist commissions or patronage. Several churches could contribute from their collections to create an interesting traveling exhibition. What a good way to become acquainted with various congregations, build awareness for their art programs, and generate goodwill among a wide audience.

There may be art collectors who are part of the congregation. Get to know them. If the church provides insurance and appropriate security, the owners may be willing to share their pieces. John Kohan, whose website (sacredpilgrim.com) features his art collection, mounts three exhibits a year for his home church, St Peter's Episcopal in Delaware, Ohio.

Some Christian universities and seminaries have art that can be rented or loaned. For example, Luther Seminary in St. Paul, Minnesota, and Calvin College in Grand Rapids, Michigan, have art collections related to the Prodigal Son that are available to faith organizations.

In addition, a number of organizations and individuals have produced art exhibits that are available for rent by churches, seminaries, universities, and small museums. These shows are an excellent resource for galleries that want to expand their offerings to viewers in an economically efficient manner. Some come from private collections that include historical works, others are juried exhibits by contemporary artists, or curated by highly qualified members of the art and faith community. *A list of exhibit rental sources is provided in Section 13.1.*

7.1 ONE-PERSON EXHIBITS

The easiest show to organize features the work of one artist. It is called a solo or one-person show. Often the committee will invite artists that it knows to exhibit. Once the gallery is established, artists outside the committee's network may request an exhibition. A fair selection process should be in place to screen applicants. Some churches solicit exhibition proposals that the committee or curator review to determine what fits the gallery's criteria and schedule. Galleries set up deadlines for submittal and once or twice a year members review the proposals. The following items are usually required in a submission:

- Letter of intent (exhibition proposal).
- General artist statement (one page).
- Artist's biography or abridged resume and contact information.
- Digital images of completed works to be included in proposed show.
- List of digital images: title, media, size, date, retail value.
- Supporting material such as catalog, books, exhibition reviews, and articles.

7.2 EXHIBITS FROM THE CONGREGATION

Showing art made by church members can be a wonderful way to honor their creative gifts and crafting skills while building a sense of community and support for the gallery. This might include a display of beautiful quilts, woodworking, stained glass, altered books or travel photography. Exhibitors could be invited to lead mini-workshops of "skill-sharing" that are videotaped for future reference.

A potential source of material is to gather symbols from the life of the congregation, such as a meaningful and fascinating exhibit of family Bibles. Tapping into the congregation to observe the liturgical calendar would be a highlight for families gathering during the holidays. For example, celebrate Easter by featuring crosses on loan from parishioners, or provide a community exhibit of creches during Christmas. To help the congregation focus on Christ's birth and incarnation during Advent, a gallery could mount a show of baby pictures or heritage christening gowns accompanied by baptismal certificates and photographs.

National holidays and cultural observances such as Martin Luther King, Jr. Day, Veterans' Day, Fourth of July, and Dia de los Muertos (Day of the Dead) are excellent opportunities to integrate the gallery with the life of the community.

One church in New York and another in Texas invited everyone to exhibit their wedding pictures. The gallery was abuzz with, "You have not changed at all," or "I would never have recognized you." Not only were the photographs displayed, but people were invited to renew wedding vows during a June Sunday worship service. In lieu of the benediction the musicians struck up *The Wedding March* and a wedding cake was served at the reception.

Another kind of display might highlight certain ministries in the church, such as objects from around the world related to the mission program. The Child Development Center at Central Presbyterian Church in Atlanta, Georgia, invited preschool children to paint pictures on 11 x 14 inch sheets of paper that were framed and hung in the church art gallery for the fortieth anniversary of the center. With imagination and a sense of adventure so much can be done to enliven the gallery's program. These displays build ownership of the gallery and develop a congregation that is comfortable in the space.

7.3 HISTORICAL ART EXHIBITS

There is a rich history of Christian art that could add to the roster of gallery shows. If someone in the congregation or a person known to the church has an art piece with a special provenance, a whole show can be built around this single work by including other artists' creations and historical artifacts that complement it in some way. Examples of historical art include pages from Medieval psalters, Renaissance drawings and etchings, architectural renderings of sacred spaces, old Mexican retablos, and specific works by important artists.

7.4 THEMATIC EXHIBITS

An exhibition organized around an idea or topic can offer a rich visual and educational experience. This kind of show really requires a curator or juror to select the art in a way that illuminates various aspects and interpretations of the theme. Church galleries have explored topics such as: creation, resurrection, light and darkness, bridges and connections, Fruit of the Spirit, parables of Jesus, images of the Virgin Mary, Noah and the Flood, work, succor, passion pilgrimage, and the Eucharist. At Menlo Park Presbyterian Church in California, a show entitled, *Mothers, Harlots, Wives and Queens: Women of the Bible*, brought together 56 visual artists and writers to imagine through art, prose, and poetry the lives of female archetypes who have inspired sermons, movies, novels, and art throughout history.

7.5 MEDIA-DRIVEN EXHIBITS

Periodically, the gallery may want to show the breadth of a certain art medium, which increases knowledge and appreciation of the art form. A curator can capitalize on the fact that the gallery is church-based by focusing on media that relate to Christian art history. Because the church has a long tradition of illuminated text, a calligraphy show could have great appeal. Icons provide a window through which the parish can more deeply appreciate other traditions and theological perspectives. Works that are based on gilding techniques reference cultural attitudes of equating gold with the divine. Folk art from Latin America, Eastern Europe, and Ethiopia present a rich heritage of Christian symbolism and faith expressions. Curated examples of "outsider art"—work created by vision-driven, self-taught evangelical artists who have no contact with the mainstream art world—can demonstrate the gift of creativity and innate expressive power.

Very often there are media-focused organizations in a region such as printmakers, book artists, photographers, collage artists, and watercolorists that can be asked to mount a show. This is a good time to focus on explaining and demonstrating techniques.

The most popular and engaging art media are often those that reflect the lives and interests of the congregants and the surrounding environment. If the church has a lot of young people making short films and exploring new technology-based media, give them a platform to share their creations. An exhibit of skateboard decks painted with religious imagery and provocative manifestos would promote intergenerational dialog. Invite neighborhood graffiti artists to work on modular panels to hang in the gallery and hire a hip-hop disc jockey to play for the opening reception. Metropolitan United Church, located in downtown Toronto, Ontario, brought together four acclaimed aerosol artists to visually demonstrate their faith and explore their spirituality on a 30 x 60 foot outside wall donated by the church.

7.6 ART OUTSIDE THE BOX EXHIBITS

A church gallery does not have to be housed in a physical space. Online, virtual galleries make art available 24:7 for worldwide viewing. These sites are curated and maintained as if they were traditional exhibits.

Pop-up galleries—temporary art installations in vacant storefronts—are appreciated in urban areas. John Knox Presbyterian Church in Seattle, Washington, collaborated with the city's arts commission to curate and install a one-day exhibit in a vacant storefront, which was attended by civic leaders and community arts administrators.

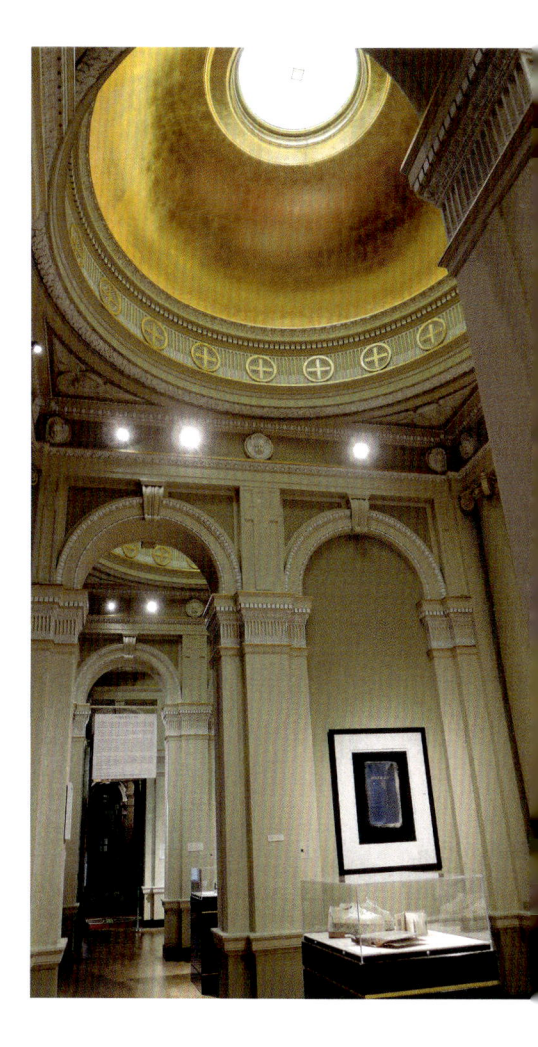

Another church in Minnesota jointly held an arts festival with a nearby ethnic Christian church that included displays of religious art, hymns, poetry, and lectures in several languages.

Some artists today work in a social practice that encompasses a range of art forms such as public art, interactive media, street performance, and art interventions. Works from this genre can be of any media and are characterized by public interaction. They are often aimed at social change and involve some empowerment of community members who come together with artists to create an artwork. Saddleback Church in Lake Forest, California, has an arts initiative called *Ex Creatis*, that includes open studio time and art installations, promoting social justice and community engagement through art.

Churches can also commission artists to create temporary installations for a specific area such as the sanctuary, exterior façade or meditation garden. Grace Cathedral in San Francisco has invited well-known culture makers to create site-specific works and events. Their 2013 artist-in-residence, Anne Patterson, produced *Graced With Light,* a music-inspired installation of 20 miles of multihued ribbons cascading from the vaulted ceiling that received over a half million "likes" on Instagram.

ORGANIZING JURIED SHOWS 8

ORGANIZING JURIED SHOWS

Juried art shows can be the most time-consuming kind of exhibit to undertake. However, a well-organized effort returns significant benefits: many artists participate in the gallery's mission, and the visual arts committee may discover artists they want to show again. Having an artist on the organizing team who has participated in juried exhibits is helpful. Many local art clubs and organizations have experience in this area and would be happy to provide counsel and advice. Don't be afraid to reach out to them.

Juried exhibits can draw from local, regional, and national artist populations. The greater the reach, the more complex and expensive it will be to produce the exhibit. Unless the church art gallery has established a national reputation and is able to process online entry forms, it is best to focus on the art community closer to home. In 1972, First United Methodist Church in Grand Rapids, Michigan, hosted its first annual art show. It is now a two-week long festival of the arts and one of the largest juried sacred art shows in the country, providing a stimulus for regional artists to explore the spiritual.

8.1 TIMELINE

About one year from the date the works will be displayed, define a timeline for all major aspects of the exhibition that relate to art selection, installation, and promotion. Include on the timeline any lectures or supporting programs that are planned. The following is a twelve-month, basic calendar for an exhibit that will be juried from CDs or online submissions. The sample does not include deadlines for closing the show, returning the art, or producing an exhibition catalog.

46 weeks	Exhibit theme is confirmed, space reserved, and jurors are chosen.
44 weeks	Prospectus is written.
40 weeks	Prospectus is distributed.
24 weeks	Exhibit information is provided to monthly magazines.
20 weeks	All art is submitted for jurying.
16 weeks	Art is selected. Artists are notified.
12 weeks	Preliminary exhibit layout is finished.
8 weeks	Publicity photographs are chosen. Website is updated.
7 weeks	Postcard is designed and sent to printers. Digital flyer is designed.
6 weeks	Press release is written and distributed to news media.
5 weeks	Information is posted to online event calendars. Signage is ordered. Art inventory list sent to insurer.
4 weeks	Digital flyer is mailed. Mailing labels and show guide are printed.
3 weeks	Postcards are mailed. Opening reception is organized. Artist binder is assembled and artist loan agreements collected.
2 weeks	Art is delivered. Labels are printed. Pedestals and walls are prepared.
1 week	Exhibition is installed.

8.2 JURORS

Find jurors who will be a catalyst for artist participation or who may offer an important viewpoint for the selection process. For example, a theologian would be an asset on the jury panel if the theme of the show has a biblical basis. An artist known for expertise in a specific medium is an obvious choice for a medium-based show. The director of a local art center, museum curator and other respected members of the art world will attract artists and lend prestige to the exhibition.

Jurors are usually paid an honorarium for their time. Honoraria range from $100 to $500 for a day's work, reflecting the professional experise of the juror and the number of entries. Some jurors will do it for free because they want to support artists and enrich the quality of life of the community, or they believe in the gallery's mission. Do not approach potential jurors until the jurying date and honorarium amount are firm. Determine beforehand if the juror will be asked to write an essay about the exhibit and attend the opening reception.

8.3 PROSPECTUS

An exhibition prospectus is also known as the call for entry. Carefully design this entry form to avoid incomplete submissions and misunderstandings. Artists will decide whether to participate based on the prospectus. The form should include information about the exhibit:

- Show title.
- Show dates.
- Show venue (full address).
- Theme description (explain the idea in a way that inspires and intrigues).
- Juror's biographical information.
- Artwork specifications (restrictions on size, weight, year made, media, subject matter).
- Information for work with special display needs (such as video projector).
- Number of entries allowed.
- How the work will be selected (images, actual work, CDs, online).
- How to submit digital images of the art for judging (examples: JPG, 72 dpi, 2 MB max).
- Fees, if any.
- Calendar (submission deadline, notification, delivery, pick up/return shipping).
- Information about insurance coverage.
- Information about who pays for shipping.
- Photography release and liability waiver.
- Name and contact information for questions.

The form should also include space for the artist's legal name (and name for publicity purposes and labels), address, email, phone number, art title, dimensions (height x width x depth), weight, materials, year made, value of the art (value data are used for insurance purposes), and an artist statement.

Send out the call for entry early enough that artists have time to prepare work for the theme. A long lead time allows continued advertising until the submission deadline. Usually the prospectus is posted in a PDF file on websites and social networks and emailed directly to artists. Sometimes churches, art organizations, art schools, and art councils will forward the information to members through their electronic newsletters. Paper copies of the prospectus can be left at artist gatherings, art stores and community art centers.

Today many art organizations use Web-based services that manage artist-application processes related to calls for entry. The service provider posts the prospectus on its website, receives the entries, handles any entry fees and sends out the selection notifications to artists when they are available. ArtCall.org, CallForEntry (CaFÉ), EntryThingy, Juried Art Services, and OnlineJuriedShows.com are examples of online juried show services. Charges, which vary according to the service, may be cost-effective for galleries conducting a wide search for artists.

8.4 SELECTION PROCESS

Jurors must read the prospectus and fully understand the exhibition theme. A juror may abstain from judging a piece that poses a conflict of interest (for example, a teacher–student relationship or family member). Only jurors should participate in the jurying process. Everyone else refrains from comments during the judging.

When selecting from actual art work, the art should be unpacked and arranged for viewing. If the juror will look at digital images, a good projection unit or computer should be set up to accommodate a slide show. A copy of all the entry forms is useful if the juror has questions about materials or the artist's interpretation of the theme. The juror should be supplied with a written list of images in the order they appear, and the approximate number of objects to be accepted.

Typically, the jury will have a quick review of all the work before the decision making begins. The images are viewed again, and the jury indicates yes, no, or undecided. A numerical system is sometimes used, such as a ranking of 1 to 7, with 1 the lowest score and 7 the highest score. The total scores for each piece are used for comparison. During the third viewing, final decisions are made. Names of the artists are revealed after the jurying is completed.

Notifications should be sent quickly to each applicant to let them know if an artwork is accepted or not. At this time, provide clear instructions for delivering the work (how, when, and where), attaching identification labels to the back, and picking up the artwork after the show closes.

HOW TO HANDLE ART

HOW TO HANDLE ART

Mounting an exhibit while protecting thousands of dollars of art inventory can be a daunting responsibility. Every gallery has an obligation to handle the art in its possession carefully and respectfully. This is not only a matter of monetary consideration, but also because the owners and artists have placed their irreplaceable property in the church's hands. This is the time to enlist the help of people in the organization who have the most experience with art.

Some churches hire professional art handlers to unpack, hang, and repack their exhibits. A local museum or art center might be a source for referrals to free lance art preparators who could assist or direct an installation The benefits of having such expertise on site may justify the expense. As an example: if an art handler can be hired at $20 per hour, and the installation takes six hours, for $120 the exhibit has been professionally installed and managed. If the church gallery does not have the budget for this, the exhibit team will need to learn methods of safely handling art objects. Setting gallery guidelines to ensure the safety of the art will minimize a host of problems. Everyone on the art installation crew should be familiar with the guidelines before starting work.

9.1 GENERAL ART HANDLING GUIDELINES
- Do not rush.
- Do not eat, drink, or smoke while handling art.
- Keep ink pens away from the installation area. Use only pencil.
- Never let wet plaster or paint come near the art.
- Put cardboard, carpet square, or another barrier between framed work and a bare floor to avoid scratching the frame.

INSTALLATION TOOL KIT

Smart gallery managers store art installation supplies in a toolbox or cart, ready to go. Depending on the hanging system, a basic installation tool kit could include:

- Apron, dust pan, and brush
- Box beam level or laser level
- Calculator
- Camera
- Claw hammer
- Cleaner formulated for acrylic
- Clean soft cloth
- Extension cord
- **Gloves** (nitrile and cotton)
- **Hardware** (picture hooks, nails, screws, and drywall anchors)
- Low tack or painter's blue tape
- Monofilament in several gauges, 20-75 pound test
- Museum putty
- Pencil, eraser, notepad
- Power Drill
- Scissors
- Screwdrivers
- Step ladder
- Tape measure
- Wall paint and paint brush
- **Wall patching materials** (putty, small spatula, sandpaper, paint)

- Always wear nitrile gloves when touching work that could be damaged by hand oils. This safeguard is especially important for textiles, metals, paper, and unglazed ceramic works. White cotton gloves (available at art and photography supply stores) may be used for handling paper and books.
- Never put a label on a frame—its sticky back will mar the frame's finish.
- Do not spray cleaner directly onto glass in a frame. Spray onto a cloth and then wipe.
- Never use glass cleaner on acrylic glazing—use cleaners formulated for plastics.
- Outside of spot-cleaning glass, do not attempt to clean artwork.
- Instruct church staff and custodians not to move installed artworks. Give them the contact information for an approved art handler if art must be moved for any reason.

9.2 RECEIVING, STORING, AND PACKING

- When crates arrive they should sit in the gallery for 24 hours to acclimate to the new temperature and humidity before opening.
- If artists are dropping off work before the installation date, have suitable space in which to safely store it.
- Do not stack framed work unless padding is placed in between; then place similar sized works front-to-front and back-to-back.
- Never stack more than five deep, and keep the art oriented in the direction it will hang.
- Use scissors to carefully cut tape and bubble wrap. Tearing off the tape destroys the wrapping and exposes tape edges that could stick to artwork.
- Do not throw away any packing material before checking for miscellaneous small pieces hidden inside.
- Keep all screws and crate hardware.
- Before handling an object, look to see if there are points of structural weakness or instability, and if it is one piece or multiples.
- Do not disassemble a work of art unless the owner has given prior approval.
- Examine the art to see if there are any areas of previous damage. Document any concerns on an Incoming Condition Report.
- Do not hang a work if it appears the hanging hardware is unreliable. Get the owner's approval before attaching new hanging devices.
- Make sure the work is tagged on the back with its title, inventory number, and artist's name. Check this against the inventory list, verifying the art is in the gallery.
- Label and store the packing material until the exhibition is over. If it is in good condition, it can be used again to return the art.
- The same person should do the unpacking and repacking, taking notes or photos so that the art is put back in the shipping container appropriately.
- At the close of the exhibit, repack the art in its original shipping containers, following any directions provided by the lender. If original shipping materials are no longer safe to use, contact the artist to discuss a solution.

9.3 MOVING ARTWORK

- Cover belt buckles with an apron. Remove jewelry and watches. Tie back long hair.
- Before moving a work, examine the route, making sure it is clear. Open doors and turn on lights in advance. Prepare the spot where the object will be put down.
- Never drag art. Always carry the art with two hands supporting a side and bottom.
- Never lift an object by its handle or a projecting part. Holding a painting by the top of its frame stresses the corners and could cause separation.
- If an object is heavy, have another person assist. Avoid passing an object from one person to another. Set it down for the next person to pick up.
- Do not lift an unframed paper by its corners. Instead put it on a clean board and cover it with another board to carry it.
- Secure work when transporting it in a cart. If it is a 3D piece, nestle the object in padding and lash it down.
- Use a ladder (not a chair!) to reach above head height. Follow the manufacturer's instructions regarding the wheel locks and extensions.

9.4 CONDITION REPORTS

An Incoming Condition Report is the accurate account of an object's condition at the time it is received. This report records the nature and location of any defect in a clear, logical, and consistent manner. If a loaned object comes into the gallery with a traveling condition report or a report provided by the artist, the staff needs to note any change that has occurred since the previous examination. An Outgoing Condition Report records any change in the object's condition before leaving the gallery.

Kinds of damage can include creases, tears, mold, insects, breakage, stains, holes, flaking paint, fading, distortion, cracks, abrasion, previous repairs, ingrained dirt, paint splatters, marks, and graffiti. An object's condition can be documented by written description, drawings, and photographs. Sometimes a combination of these three methods is necessary.

When preparing to do a condition report, it will be helpful to have good lighting, digital camera, pencil, paper, and nitrile gloves. There are many different forms that a condition report can follow, but all will provide the following basic information:

- Exhibition title.
- Exhibition sponsor and contact information.
- Date of report.
- Examiner's name.
- Artist name and contact information.
- Title or inventory number of the artwork.
- Type of shipping container and packing materials.
- Dates of art arrival and unpacking.
- Description of the artwork (media, dimensions, number of parts).
- Precise description of damage and its location.

9.5 WHEN DAMAGE OCCURS

Even with careful handling, accidents can happen: sometimes a gallery visitor is at fault, a hanger device can fail, or the roof leaks. Photograph any damage, fill out an Outgoing Condition Report, and notify the lender within 48 hours. Carefully collect broken pieces and put them in a covered box or sealed bag. Decide if the work should be removed from the exhibit. Do not attempt to make any repairs without the consent of the owner.

How the damage is addressed depends on the gallery's policies, insurance terms, and artist/lender agreement. Who files the claim depends on who purchased the insurance and when the damage occurred.

Open all crates within 24 hours of delivery. If damage occurred during shipping, save the container in which the art was shipped and notify the shipper when the damage is discovered. If it is clear at the time of delivery that a box or crate is damaged, ask the driver to contact the company in your presence. Fill out an Incoming Condition Report and notify the lender within 48 hours.

If an artist claims that the work is returned damaged, and the gallery was responsible for the return shipping, ask the artist to save the exterior and interior shipping boxes, including the label and tracking numbers. The shipper and insurer will want to check the condition of the boxes and packing materials. Decide who will process the insurance claim, and confirm that the artist will provide a written description and photos of the damage. Keep copies of all correspondence.

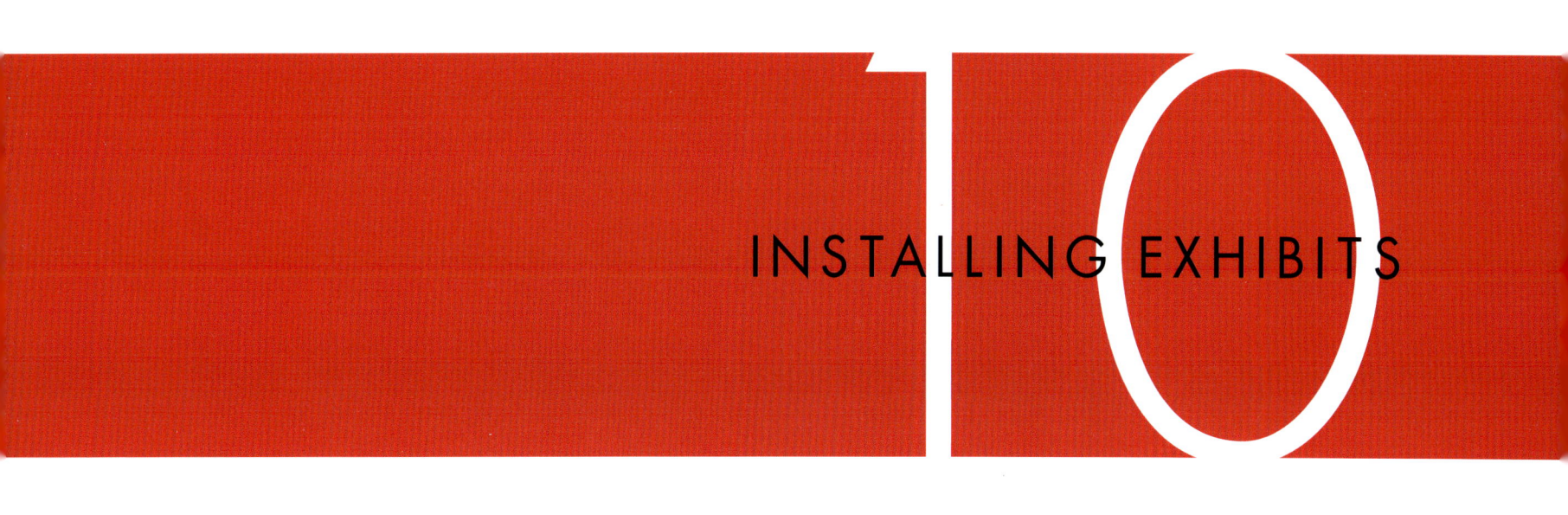

10 INSTALLING EXHIBITS

INSTALLING EXHIBITS

Excitement and pressure increase when the time finally arrives to install the art show. All those months of planning, curating, and promoting now culminate in the task of mounting the display. Typically, the installation team goes into action one week before the opening. Walls and pedestals may need to be built, patched, or painted. The gallery space may need to be cleared of furniture and its normal clutter. Technical equipment must be checked and burned out light bulbs replaced.

How art is displayed in the gallery is called the exhibit layout or design. Next to selecting the artwork, this plan is probably the most important aspect of mounting an art show. The design determines how people move from one piece to another and the connections they make between the works and with the architectural space. The arrangement, spacing, and lighting of the artwork guide viewers to intellectually engage with the theme and affect their experience and emotions.

10.1 ARRANGING ART

A floor plan of the gallery space is a valuable aid for designing exhibits. Rendered to-scale on a standard 8.5 x 11-inch sheet of paper, the plan should include wall and ceiling height measurements, doors, windows, electrical outlets, and any structures that would affect the art layout. Note areas that have bad lighting or difficult viewer access. Make multiple copies of the floor plan, and keep an original in a paper file or on a computer.

Some curators build 3D models of the exhibition out of mat board or foam core and attach scale reproductions of the artwork with removable adhesive. If the gallery is large and the organization expects to mount complicated exhibits, the curator may want a 3D gallery planning software program that creates a virtual mock up of an exhibit and allows easy changes.

There are a variety of computer applications, from expensive and complicated to free and simple. Architects and interior designers often have expertise in computer-aided design. An architect at First Presbyterian Church in Hilton Head, South Carolina, recreates the gallery's floor plan using a SketchUp program to show the layout and placement of art in the exhibition. For the majority of church-based galleries, a curator with vision, paper, pencil, and calculator can accomplish excellent results.

The main challenge is to create a composition that lets each piece have a presence within a harmonious whole. The art arrangement should mediate relationships between the individual works. If the gallery is housed in a significant architectural space, the curator must also consider the synergy between the art and the building's features. Artworks exhibited in an area used for worship require sensitive placements that support rather than detract from the liturgical and religious activities that happen there.

To plan the installation, study the art in advance. Print digital images of the works and use them with the floor plan to imagine their placement in the gallery. Do the math to ensure the art will fit the space. Final decisions can be made after the art is unpacked and leaned against the walls.

The exhibit layout directs both the visual flow and the physical traffic flow of people through the space. Note the exits and entrances that determine the direction people are most likely to move. Be aware of how natural light will change throughout the day. Other points to consider:

- What will catch visitors' attention as they enter and exit the room?

- Place pedestals so traffic flow is not impeded.
- Highlight one work in a prominent place, and use this image in promotional materials.
- Place the show title sign so it is visible without interfering with the art.
- Disperse bright colored-art throughout the room, or put in spaces that need focal points.
- Minimize uncomfortable juxtapositions between frame styles and colors.
- Allow space for viewers to step back to observe large works.
- Analyze shapes and sizes of works in relation to the room and to each other.
- Consider the scale and relation of 3D objects and pedestals to other works.
- Seek similarities in subject matter, shapes, lines, patterns, and color.
- Try grouping works by subject matter or media.
- Consider if there is an innate theme progression or a timeline.
- Have fun finding unexpected relationships, such as an image of a window hung near a real window.

SEEING THE UNSEEN   SECTION 10

10.2 SPACING ART

Space for showing two-dimensional art is measured in linear feet. Artwork is always measured height x width, width being the linear measurement. Make sure to differentiate when communicating with artists if they are to supply outside (frame edges) or inside (art) measurements. To estimate how many linear feet of artwork may be hung and allow for space between works, divide the number of linear feet in half. For example, 100 linear feet will accommodate about 50 linear feet of artwork. More art may be displayed by stacking or creating groupings of small pieces.

Exhibition space for three-dimensional artwork is measured in square feet. So a 15 x 40 gallery would have 600 square feet for display. A sculpture's size determines how much space is necessary to view each side. The larger the scale, the more space it needs. Even a small sculpture may require extra space to accommodate large crowds, such as a gallery that also functions as the church lobby.

Pedestals are generally used for displaying 3D objects. Typically they are simple cubes and pillars made out of plywood, and painted the same neutral color so they don't detract from the art. For aesthetic and safety purposes, match the pedestal height and size to the artwork. Items should never overlap the top of a pedestal. A large pedestal will overpower a single small piece. Clear plastic boxes set on top of pedestals—called vitrines—may be needed to cover small objects or a work that needs extra protection.

In some cases, it may be advisable to build temporary walls that help move viewers through the space or create separate display areas. Wall color, dramatic lighting, and positioning a powerful artwork are all techniques to control visual flow and traffic patterns.

The goal is for each object in the display to be appreciated and studied. If there are too many works, the exhibit may become a blur of visual information. Do not feel compelled to fill the room. There are, of course, always exceptions to the less-is-more rule. "Salon-style" displays that stack art—sometimes right up to the ceiling—originated in Paris in the 1700s. However, unless the exhibition's intent is to create an overpowering image montage, it is always best to give each piece of art its due.

10.3 HANGING ART

Artwork that is hung too high can be a problem for viewing by some, including children and people in wheelchairs. If the art is installed too low, others will have to bend over to focus on it. Art is usually hung with the central focus at about five feet. This means that the center of each work would be at the same height (56-60 inches) from the floor. If all the work is very large, align their bottom edges at the same distance from the floor.

To hang a wired artwork at 60 inches:

- Find the center of the wall space where the art will hang.
- Make an intersecting mark (the "eye level mark") at 60 inches from the floor.
- Measure the distance from the top of the art to the wire (the "wire drop").
- Extend a tape measure to the height of the art. Place the middle of the tape on the eye level mark. Find the wire drop measure on the tape. This is the point where the bottom of the picture hook is hammered into the wall.

Although it's tempting to hang lightweight artwork on nails, picture hangers are a much safer method. A hanger is designed so that the nail goes into the wall at an angle and stays in that position. The advantage for an art gallery is that hangers make a very small hole that's easy to patch when the art is removed. A set of reusable Floreat hangers made by Ziabicki or OOK will be a good investment. These brass plated steel hooks with tempered steel nails can hold up to 100 pounds and are used by many professional art installers.

Always use a hook that is rated for the weight of the artwork and allow an ample safety margin. Large paintings are rarely hung with wire, but on large D-rings or strap hangers attached to both sides of the frame back and slipped over screws or hooks inserted in the wall. As a rule of thumb, drywall can safely accommodate an 80-pound object that is outfitted with D-rings. Sometimes a heavy artwork will be equipped with a French cleat hanger. This type of hardware is composed of two long strips of interlocking metal or wood. One side is screwed into the wall, and the other is attached to the back of the artwork.

If the piece is heavier than 100 pounds, use anchors with the screws. There are a variety of types including plastic drywall anchors, metal screw mounts, expanding metal screws, and mortar/concrete anchors. Molly and toggle bolts are permanent and should not be used for rotating art shows. When removed they leave large holes that are difficult to patch. For very heavy artworks it is best to drive screws or nails into the wall studs. A vertical stud on 16-inch centers will carry several hundred pounds if the object is properly screwed through the sheathed wall. When suspending objects from ceiling drywall, drive hooks or screws into the ceiling rafters.

To hang artwork on picture molding:

- Put a small piece of blue painter's tape on the wall, 60 inches from floor.
- One person stands on a ladder, another holds the art approximately where it will be placed.
- Put the S-hook over the molding.
- Insert weight-appropriate monofilament through both D-rings and pull ends up a bit higher than the S-hook. Cut.
- Join the ends with an ordinary knot, followed by an overhand knot. Pull the long ends of line in opposite directions to ensure knot is firm. Arrange knot so that it is behind the frame.
- Slip monofilament over the S-hook. While one person supports the art, the person on the ladder wraps the line over the hook's bottom until center of artwork is at the 60-inch mark.

To hang artwork on a track and hanger system, follow the manufacturer's instructions regarding weight loads and adjusting the rod and clips.

Once the art is installed, attach identification labels to the wall with rolls of low-tack tape (painter's blue tape) or removable adhesive putty. They are usually placed to the right of the object and at the same height from the floor throughout the exhibit. Place sculpture labels on the pedestals or the nearest wall or floor. Museum putty can also be used to secure objects to the pedestals and brace wall frames so they do not tilt.

10.4 ADJUSTING LIGHTS

After all the artwork and identification labels have been put in place, the gallery lights can be adjusted so that art and signage are sufficiently illuminated and the appropriate mood or ambiance of the room is created with light and shadow. Lighting is an art in itself that often requires subjective decisions. The curator or artist may want to have the final choice. A ladder is essential and work gloves are useful for handling hot bulbs and canisters.

The most important lighting mistakes to avoid are strong shadow forms and light patterns on walls and ceiling; undesirable reflections and shadows on the artwork; cast shadows on adjacent objects; and glare from lamps directed into viewers' faces.

Two-dimensional art hung on a wall is usually lighted at a 30-degree angle. A steeper angle will highlight surface texture, but the tradeoff is muted color, and a deep frame will cast a shadow on the work. In the reverse, shallow angles enhance color but flatten textures and reflect glare. Adjust the beam spread to cover the artwork and allow for spill light to illuminate the identification label. Multiple spots are needed to create even lighting across larger works of art.

As a rule, spatial art should be lighted from a longer distance than pictorial art so the light reaches more than the top of the piece. Sculpture is often illuminated with a combination of diffused and directional lighting. Projecting light beams from two directions will highlight the shape and texture of the object, creating shadows that express depth. Keep the light beam spread within the mass of the object. For glass artwork, put lights in the front, back, and both sides to bring out the transparent qualities of the material.

Keep the lighting subdued for audio visual installation, and try to avoid highly directional lights that could cause annoying reflected glare on the screens.

Once the lights are adjusted, it's a good idea to measure the light levels. The exhibit area should be bright enough that viewers can appreciate the art, but low enough to avoid damaging it. The intensity of visible light in a given area is measured in lux units. 50-100 lux is considered the maximum allowable light level for artworks containing fabric,

10.5 DOCUMENTING THE DISPLAY

Take time to photograph the installation for future reference and for promotional purposes. The goal here isn't to photograph the individual artworks as much as it is to record how the art was arranged in the gallery. If the visual arts team has the resources, procure the services of a photographer who has the camera lens, computer software, and skills to shoot interior spaces. A dynamic image that captures the mood of the lighting, controls the visual perspective, and conveys a "wow" factor can be used on the gallery's website and other forms of publicity. Good photo records are also helpful for new curators and installers in the gallery's future.

It's also a great idea to take photographs during the reception or at a time when visitors are engaged with the artworks. Look for opportunities to show families and individuals from a range of ages and backgrounds enjoying the art exhibit.

non-colorfast pigments, paper, and vintage materials. Up to 150 lux is acceptable for oil paintings, photographs, and wood objects. Metal, stone, glass, and ceramics are considered light fast.

A variety of light meters are available from photography, lighting, and office equipment suppliers. There are even downloadable apps that allow a smart phone to be used as a lux meter.

ENGAGING VIEWERS

ENGAGING VIEWERS

Art museums take seriously their education role. They employ a wide array of methods to make learning about art fun and stimulating for everyone, from children to advanced scholars. Much of the success of a church-related gallery is connected to the educational materials and supporting programs that are offered to viewers of different ages and cultural backgrounds. The audience for a religious-themed art exhibit will also have varying levels of knowledge regarding art and theology.

Art is a visual language in which many are not fluent. It is not uncommon to hear someone say, "I don't know much about art, but I know what I like." What they are really saying is that they like what they know. With insights into the artist's intent, techniques and art materials, as well as helpful explanations about subject matter and its spiritual significance, viewers can more deeply appreciate the artwork and its relevance. Art education tools include fundamentals, such as wall signs and art labels plus enrichment programs, such as artist lectures, exhibit catalogs, and teaching curricula. The scope of what can be done to support the art exhibit is limited only by the creativity of the visual arts committee.

11.1 WALL SIGNAGE

"Branding" the show with a title enhances publicity and helps direct interpretation. The curatorial team should select a title that captures attention and ignites interest. The complete title should be used consistently throughout the exhibition: gallery wall, exhibit guide, press release, and postcard announcement. A sign with the name of the show displayed near the entrance offers visitors a hint of what lies ahead. Vinyl letters, which can be bought from sign shops and online vendors, are attached to paper that is placed against the wall and transferred by rubbing the surface. As an alternative, gallery staff can put the title on a large self-adhesive label, frame a

LABEL EXAMPLES:

Christ on the Cross
1936
Georges Rouault
Aquatint
25 5/8 x 19 5/8 inches

Georges Rouault
Christ on the Cross
1936
Aquatint
25 5/8 x 19 5/8 inches

computer-printed poster, or order a foam-core mounted sign from a copy shop.

An information panel near the gallery entrance might include an image from the show, intent of the exhibit, short description, and information about the artists. Keep the text of the sign brief and the print large, so that visitors can scan it without stopping the traffic flow into the room.

Each art object must be identified with a label. The label includes title, artist name, medium, and sometimes size and date created. Usually in a church setting the price of an artwork is not put on a wall mounted label. The title can be italicized, put in bold, all caps, or larger text than other information. Distinguishing the title is particularly important to help the viewer identify the subject and connect to the content of the work. Make all the labels the same width and out of a consistent material such as clear acetate, foam-core mounted, or heavy weight paper. Choose an easy-to-read font style, no smaller than a 14-point font. Free software is available online for popular label brands.

Interpretive labels are great educational tools because they offer information that might not be obvious to the viewer. Along with the

Nuit de Noël
Henri Matisse (1869–1954)
Lithograph, 1954
15 x 10.5 inches

Nuit de Noël celebrates the Christmas story in a blue domed panel filled with playful stars on top of other colorful floral and abstract shapes. All nature sings of the Christ child's birth.

Matisse was one of the greatest colorists of the twentieth century. Late in his life and with a serious illness Matisse was too weak to stand at an easel, so he created a new art form called "cutouts." Using large scissors, he cut shapes out of brightly colored papers—plant forms, stars, and decorative designs. He said he was drawing with scissors and sculpting with color.

required facts, they have a few sentences about the artist's intent, explain the symbolism, or place the art in a historical context. An interpretive label might also include biblical texts associated with the art as a way to invite the viewer to reflect on the artist's insights and inspiration. If the exhibit includes many artists, the information that is submitted should be edited for uniformity, grammar, and length. Keep the length of interpretive labels less than 150 words. Otherwise, visitors will spend more time reading than looking at the art.

11.2 INFORMATIONAL MATERIALS

A gallery guide is a document that highlights specific works or encourages visitors to engage the art. It could take the form of a laminated page that remains in the gallery, a photocopied handout, or a brochure. At a minimum the guide should have a short description of the show, the artist's background, list of works in the exhibit, and an image. Offering the viewer a simple take-home handout is important because it extends the memory of the exhibition.

With basic digital tools, the gallery can create an audio tour of the exhibit and upload it to a website, blog, or iTunes. Put information about the audio tour in the promotional material, or provide a Quick Response Code (QR code) on the gallery signage. People could listen to the tour before visiting the gallery or download it to a portable media player with a headset for walking through the exhibit.

A valuable aid for visitors is a three-ring binder filled with supportive information on each artist in the show. This might include a biography, resume, news articles, and additional photographs of art. A show binder can also include the curator's and artist's statements, and it is a discrete place to list prices or the artist's contact information.

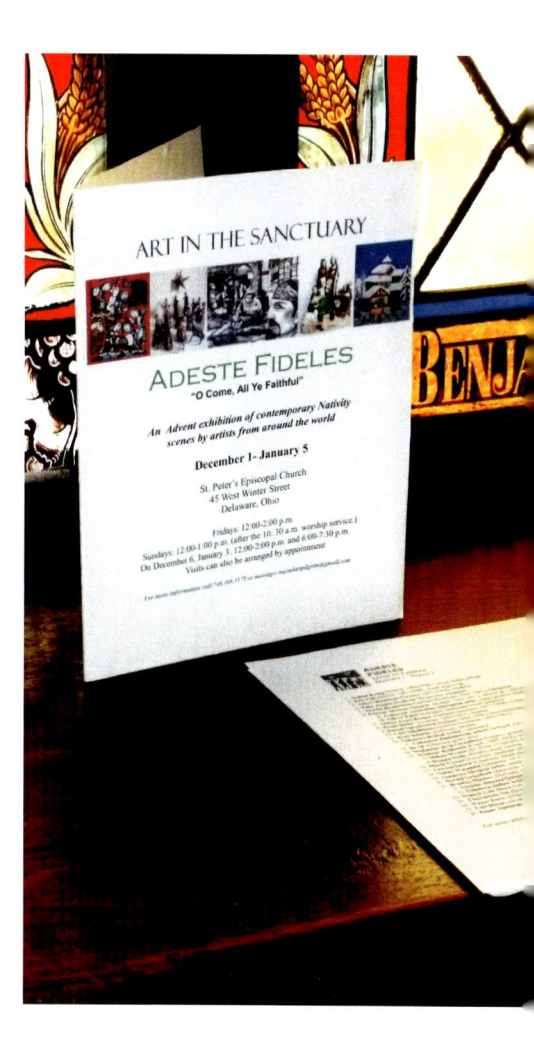

A book, or exhibition catalog, with images of the artwork and text about the theme can be a lasting record for artists, gallery, and visitors. Such a project may require several thousand dollars. However, catalogs can be produced with no upfront costs through one of the popular print-on-demand websites such as Blurb and Lulu. These self-publishing services provide free software for designing the book. Once the book is uploaded to the website, anyone in the world can buy copies in both paperback or hardback formats. The site manages the purchase and distributes the book, even for single orders.

11.3 VISITOR INTERACTION

It is important to include in every show a method for visitor response. Many exhibition venues provide a guestbook for people to sign and record comments. One gallery in Dallas, Texas, asked a question on a wall, and allowed visitors to place their answers on Post-It notes. Another invited people to write comments on tags and hang them on a treelike structure that related to the theme of the exhibit. Not only do visitors appreciate the opportunity to respond to the art, but their comments and opinions will be useful for evaluating the gallery's programs.

Opportunities for visitor education can bring the art to life. For example, a carved wood block displayed next to a print explains how it was made. A needlepoint exhibit might include a small work-in-progress that can be held and turned over. A video can teach about the artist or the artistic process. A table display of books or magazines related to the exhibition is another way to engage viewers. Put labels on the covers that say, "Gallery Copy—Do Not Remove."

Tailoring information specifically for young people builds audiences for the future. A card with fun questions can lead children through the exhibit, like a treasure hunt, looking for the answers. Families will appreciate a take-home art project related to the theme that everyone can do together, or a colorful booklet with Bible stories that are referenced in the exhibit. A Sunday School class could organize a visit to the gallery, followed by an art project for the children to respond to what they have seen.

11.4 TOURS AND DOCENTS

Some churches offer guided tours at specific times. One church in Ohio advertises that the gallery will be open to the public and a guided tour given each Friday at noon. A monthly tour after a worship service could serve as a catalyst for group discussions and community building.

Other churches have hosts available whenever the gallery is open. First Presbyterian Church Gallery in Portland, Oregon, organizes volunteers who open the gallery, welcome visitors, answer any questions, and invite people to sign the guestbook. Docents can also be available to lead tours through the exhibit for special groups such as a class of school children, seminary faculty, or a women's auxiliary. It is a good idea for the show's curator to meet with the docents as a group for a walkthrough of the exhibit so that everyone is equally informed.

11.5 RECEPTIONS AND ARTIST TALKS

A common practice in the art world are receptions for the opening and/or closing of an art exhibit. Many church galleries hold a reception immediately following a Sunday service. Others may coordinate their exhibits to coincide with a monthly "art walk" night when all the art galleries in the city open their doors to visitors.

A reception is a great opportunity for the church to extend an invitation to the surrounding community. The event could be as simple as punch and cookies, or it could involve entertainment and other special activities. When West Valley Presbyterian Church in Cupertino, California, opened an exhibit of angel imagery during the Christmas season, it invited the neighborhood to come over for a harp concert and holiday refreshments. Other churches have enhanced their art receptions with string quartets, vocalists, dance performances, and poetry readings.

It is beneficial to have the exhibiting artists attend the opening. Many people appreciate the opportunity to meet the artists and ask questions. Sometimes an artist will be invited to give a short talk, sharing personal insights into the work.

11.6 LECTURES AND FIELD TRIPS

A great way to expand the congregation's appreciation of a show is to offer a lecture that places the work in historic and cultural perspective. Apostles Anglican Church in Lexington, Kentucky, had two lectures during the exhibit, *Marc Chagall and the Bible*. A member of the congregation who is an art historian gave an introductory lecture to open the show, and a Jewish professor from the nearby university gave a lecture at the closing of the exhibition. Over 150 people attended with a major portion of them coming from the Jewish community.

As part of the exhibition, *Highly Favored: Images of the Virgin Mary,* a church in New England had a symposium where theologians from Catholic, Protestant, Orthodox, and Muslim traditions presented their views. The art provided a way to understand and appreciate the differences and similarities within these faith communities.

Over time, a gallery develops a following of individuals who love the arts. An organized trip to a museum expands the group's educational experience. Depending on location, this can be a quick trip downtown, or an all day bus ride to a major museum that has a particularly relevant exhibition. Consider arranging a guided tour followed by lunch when participants can engage in a lively discussion about art and faith. One of the ultimate experiences that a gallery might offer would be a travel abroad opportunity to visit significant venues of historical religious art.

11.7 CLASSES AND WORKSHOPS

A class on theology and art would go a long way in cultivating an understanding of the importance of image in spiritual formation. To augment its gallery program, Visions Gallery in Albany, New York, offered a monthly class exploring the history of Christian art. A book group was formed in another gallery to read Jaroslov Pelikan's *Jesus Through the Centuries*, as a way to more fully understand the historical changes in art.

Any number of workshops can be organized that will develop a greater appreciation for the visual arts. An iconographer could give a workshop on icon writing when the gallery is displaying icons. During Lent one group had a workshop for children and adults that taught traditional Ukrainian *panska* egg painting. Inviting an art collector to give a presentation on the importance of being caretakers of our visual history can ignite a passion for art collection.

11.8 DEVOTIONALS AND SERMONS

When an exhibit coincides with a liturgical season, the church could create devotional materials reflecting on the artwork, which could be distributed in booklet form or by email to congregants. Bidwell Presbyterian Church in Chico, California, asked members of the congregation to write meditations on pieces of art that were displayed in the gallery during Lent. Some churches have used the art as a catalyst or a central part of the minister's sermon series, using an image from the exhibit as the cover of the worship brochure. The pastor of First Baptist Church of Scottsdale, Arizona, used one piece each week from a show on the *Passion of Christ* to enlighten the text.

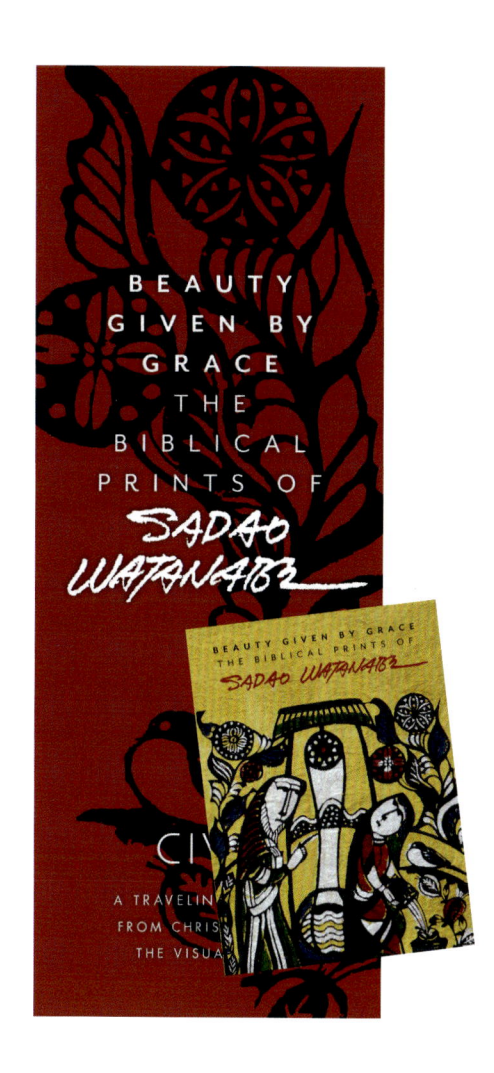

12

PROMOTION AND PUBLICITY

PROMOTION AND PUBLICITY

To raise awareness of the gallery's programs, educate about the intersection of image and Spirit, and gain a following of people interested in displays of artistic expressions of faith, the gallery will want to conduct ongoing communications with its key audiences. Publicity efforts could include a variety of activities, depending on the gallery's focus. It would be helpful to have someone with marketing experience on the gallery advisory team. Larger churches may have communications staff who will assist with the gallery's announcements within the church and to the public. Exhibiting artists are usually happy to send the show's publicity materials to their personal contacts and post on their internet sites.

12.1 INTERNET PRESENCE

A gallery website or easily accessible page on the church's website is essential. Here the gallery's mission statement and exhibition news should be available for congregants, artists, the wider faith community, and general public. If filled with great photos and engaging copy, the website will help to brand the gallery and attract visitors.

A blog is an effective tool for increasing public awareness and driving people to the gallery website. Content must be useful and updated on a consistent basis. Write about the gallery's news events, but also make it a point to inspire, educate, and inform readers about broader issues of visual art and faith. Tell stories! For example, artist interviews, book reviews, images of a religious art exhibit at the local museum, and posts from a Christian art conference will be appreciated by readers and make the gallery's program relevant. An effective blog will help potential patrons, partners, and artists learn about the gallery. WordPress and Blogger are established platforms for people new to blogging. Because they are easy to use, you will use them more often. Consider adding an RSS feed (Rich Site Summary) to the website and blog that alerts subscribers to news as soon as it is posted.

With a feed, people receive timely updates without having to visit the website.

Social networking media, such as Facebook, Twitter, Instagram, and Tumblr, are exceptional platforms for engaging with gallery fans, particularly younger demographic groups. People increasingly use social media to keep up to date on gallery exhibits, meet each other, and most important, share comments and opinions that can guide the gallery's programming. The visual arts committee should develop a social media content strategy and put it on a calendar. Think of ways to "curate" content by linking not only to the gallery's blog and website, but also to other sites, articles, people, and events that are relevant to the gallery's mission.

Creating a short (less than two minutes) video is a great way to let people experience and enjoy a gallery exhibit long after it has closed. Free or low cost apps are available for the iPhone and iPad that allow anyone to shoot, edit, add licensed music and stylish effects, and share a movie clip on the gallery's website, social media, and a YouTube or Vimeo account. Three popular apps for this are Cameo, Magisto, and Adobe Premiere Clip.

12.2 GALLERY CONTACT LISTS

Vital to the success and growth of a gallery is keeping in regular contact with those who are interested in its programs. At the end of every exhibit, transfer the names and addresses of people who left their information in the guestbook into a software program that can be used to print address labels and electronically distribute important announcements.

To implement a publicity program, it is necessary to identify the appropriate news media that might be interested in an upcoming art exhibit at the gallery. It is helpful to have the contact information for people at each of these sources and to know their deadlines for receiving news. Potential news sources include:

- Community event calendars.
- Art and entertainment sections of newspapers.
- Art magazines.
- Religion editors.
- Blogs about art and faith.
- Newsletters of local churches.
- Denominational magazines.

12.3 NEWSLETTER

A newsletter is a great way to keep in touch and nurture relationships. If the church already has one—electronic or print—make sure that the gallery has a regular feature in it.

Use a newsletter to update fans about the gallery's exhibits and provide information that is so good people will share it, save it, and look forward to each issue. Write about art, art history, theology, topics related to an exhibit, how to collect and care for art—anything that will keep readers' attention over the long run.

There are many affordable and free online email marketing services, such as MailChimp and FineArtAmerica.com to help simplify the process of designing and distributing a digital newsletter that is professional and legal (automated opt-out function). Electronic newsletters can be sent more frequently because they are less expensive to produce and recipients can forward them without much effort. On the downside, they are easy to ignore and not all the gallery's constituents are email users. Advantages of a print newsletter: they have a longer shelf life and can be left in the gallery for visitors to enjoy.

12.4 NEWS RELEASE

If the gallery wants to reach beyond its own congregation, it is important to have a news release for each show. The church communications department also needs good information to make announcements in its internal publications. A release should be distributed electronically to news media according to their submission guidelines. Reporters prefer that the release is in the body of an email, not as an attachment. Mail the release 4-6 weeks before the opening.

Attach to the email one or two high-resolution photographs in JPG format. Select a photo that will reproduce well even if printed as a small black and white image on cheap newsprint. It may not be the strongest work in the show, but it will grab the reader's attention on a busy page of competing pictures and text. Usually higher contrast images work best.

Start the release with the contact information of someone who will be available to reporters, followed by a succinct headline, "Trinity Gallery Presents *The Rains Came Down: Noah and the Ark.*" Summarize the whole story in the first paragraph (who, what, when, where), and give supporting details in subsequent paragraphs. A typical news release will contain:

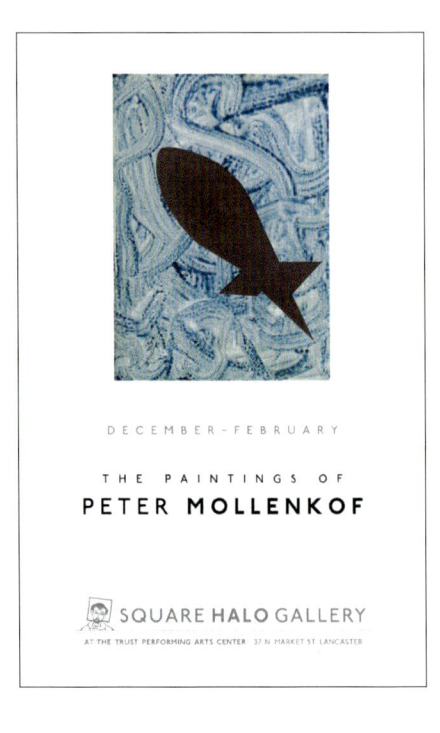

- Contact information (name, phone, email).
- Headline.
- Exhibition dates.
- General description of the show and supporting programs.
- Quotation from the artist or curator.
- Brief artist's biography.
- Specific descriptions of one or two pieces in the show.
- Information on the gallery, hours, and location.

12.5 ANNOUNCEMENTS

To bring attention to a special show or event, produce a printed invitation or postcard. Go for great color and quality paper. The announcement will be seen by people who never get to see the show. A variety of online vendors, such as PsPrint, Modern Postcard, and Vistaprint, provide electronic design templates and printing services at reasonable rates with quick turnaround. Send postcards to the gallery contact list and leave them in venues that accept community art announcements, such as bookstores, art stores, galleries, museums, and cultural centers.

Today many galleries send their exhibit announcements electronically, which saves time and money. Even if the show postcard is attached to an email, the text of the announcement must be in the body of the message so that the recipient has the information without having to open the attachment.

A printed or photocopied flyer can be displayed on church and community bulletin boards. Some storefronts will allow posters in their windows. Always ask permission before posting if there is any doubt, and don't forget to remove them when the show is over.

12.6 ADS, INTERVIEWS, AND REVIEWS

For special art events that are attractive to a wide public, consider purchasing advertisements in newspapers, art magazines, and online news sites.

Local radio and television stations and other news media may be interested in interviews with an artist or the church's art director. It isn't easy to obtain an interview because journalists receive a great many pitches daily from companies and people wanting press coverage. Before making your pitch, work up a concise, creative, and compelling request for the reporter's time and attention, such as how the exhibit relates to a current political issue or historical anniversary, its importance to a reader demographic, or why the work of a particular artist is significant.

Finally, get to know the art critics in your area. These people function as reporters, writing articles in which they analyze the content and quality of an artist's work and art exhibitions. Typically critics do not do reviews on request. It is best to send the press information and let the art and theme speak for themselves.

13
USEFUL RESOURCES

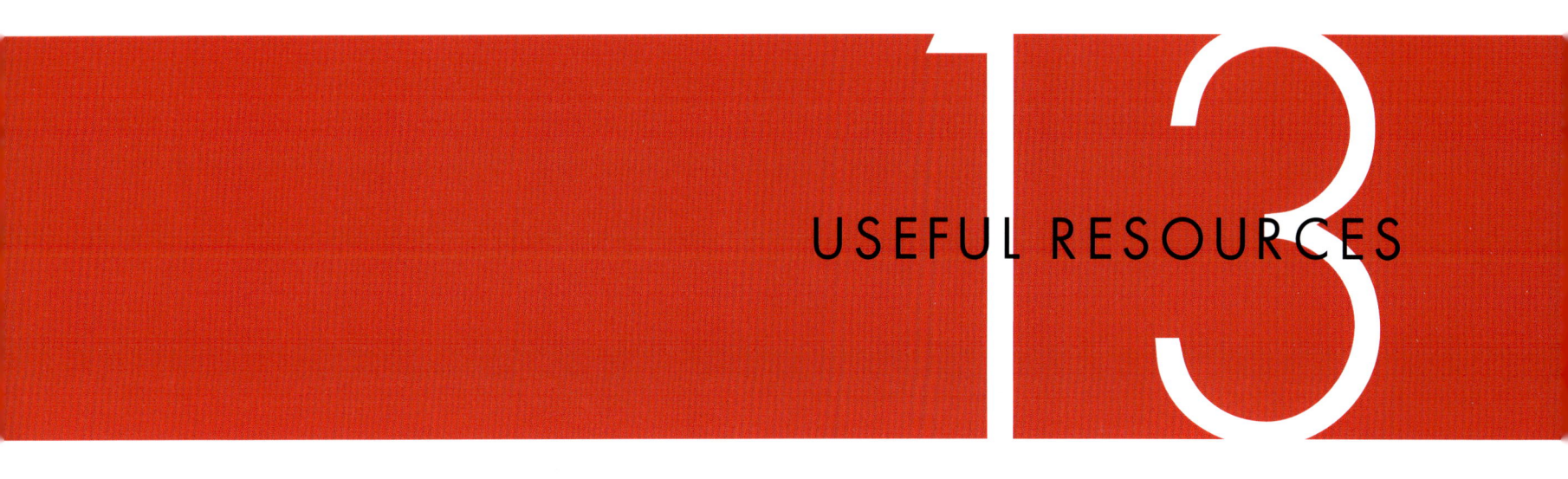

USEFUL RESOURCES

13.1 CURATED EXHIBITS

Bowden Collections
BOWDENCOLLECTIONS.COM

Bowden Collections rents quality exhibitions that are directly related to the Bible. These shows typically include between 25 to 30 paintings, prints or sculptures, making them small enough for most church related galleries. Shows include: *Eden to Eternity: Biblical Molas from the San Blas Islands; The Rains Came Down: Noah and the Ark; Otto Dix: Matthäus Evangelium; Jesus: Good Shepherd and Lamb of God;* and *Marc Chagall and the Bible*. The site gives descriptions, shows images of works offered and includes a booking schedule for each show.

CIVA | Christians in the Visual Arts
CIVA.ORG

For more than 25 years, Christians in the Visual Arts has produced a variety of traveling exhibitions such as, *Beauty Given by Grace: The Biblical Prints of Sadao Watanabe; Art + Text; The Artist and the Bible: 20th Century Works on Paper; Ordained to Create: The Self Taught Art of Southern Preachers, Prophets and Visionaries; Touch, Anoint, Heal; Come to the Table;* and *WORK: Curse or Calling?* Its website describes the exhibitions, availability, and rental terms. Shows are typically rented for a two-month period and include educational and promotional materials that support the exhibit.

Nagel Institute for the Study of World Christianity
CALVIN.EDU/NAGEL

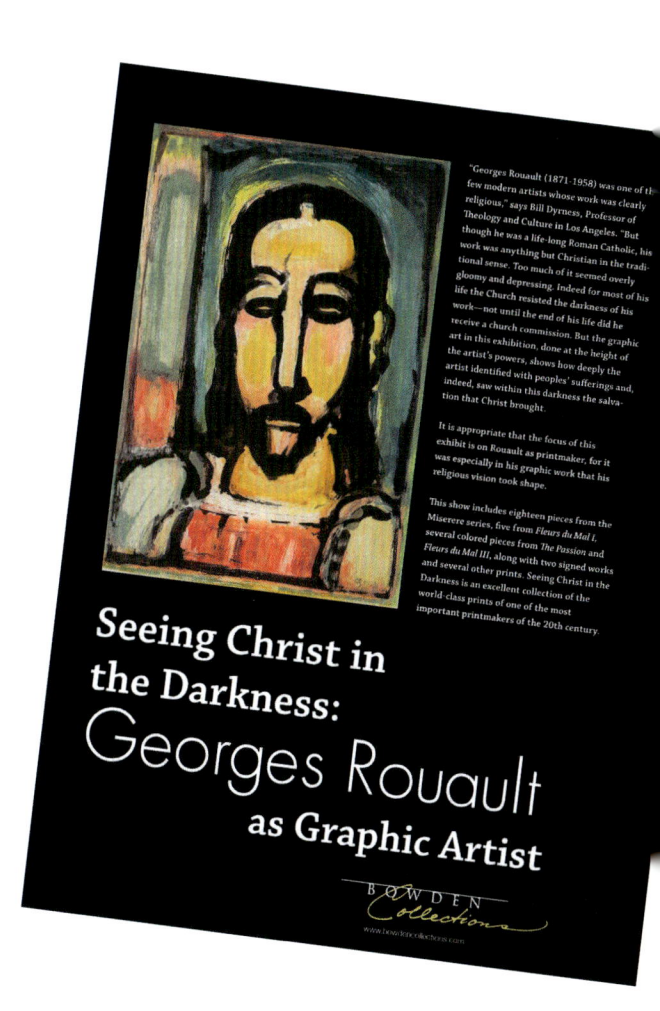

The Nagel Institute sponsors Gospel and Culture Seminars in international settings such as Indonesia and South Africa, to enable North American art faculty and local artists to explore together contemporary art that references cultural heritage and current social issues. Art exhibitions produced through the collaboration include ***Charis: Boundary Crossings*** and ***Between the Shadow and the Light.*** The Institute works with the booking venue to develop creative and thought-provoking programming for different audiences. The website provides information on current offerings and contact information for inquiries.

Masterpiece Christian Fine Arts Foundation
MCFINEARTSFOUNDATION.ORG

The foundation's mission is to visually communicate Christ to culture through traditional fine art. Masterpiece Christian Arts exhibits are typically composed of 45–90 biblically themed artworks by contemporary illustrators such as Thomas Blackshear, Ron DiCianni, Michael Dudash, Chris Hopkins, and Frank Ordaz. Touring exhibits have included ***Let There Be Light*** and ***Birds, Beasts, & Beauty–Genesis to Revelation Alliance with Animals.*** The foundation will work directly with churches and organizations to customize an exhibit or book an available curated show.

Seeds Fine Art Exhibits
SEEDSFINEART.ORG

Seeds, founded in 2003, organizes art exhibits of conceptual art by contemporary artists. It seeks to generate dialogs between art and the viewer and support the artist's call to create through exhibits that visually explore God's love, hope and salvation. Past exhibits have included, ***Dark Inheritance: Purposeful Dislocation; Out of the Ashes; Succour;*** and ***Voices.*** The curatorial team is available to do custom exhibits, dealing directly between the artists and the venue.

13.2 ART EXHIBITION TUTORIALS

Affordable Exhibition Design
by Frances Zamora Mola
ISBN-13: 978-0-0619-6882-2

This is a reference book for imaginative, practical and budget-friendly exhibition designs. Each project is selected for its aesthetic appeal, affordable construction costs, use of re-usable resources, and ease of implementation. Sketches, models and photographs reveal the process behind each project's construction.

American Alliance of Museums
The organization supports museums and individuals by developing standards and best practices. The members-only Resource Library provides over 2,000 how-to guides, articles and tools on a wide range of topics.
aam-us.org

Exhibit Labels: An Interpretive Approach
by Beverly Serrell
ISBN-13: 978-0-7619-9106-9
The book provides guidelines on the process of exhibit label planning, writing, design, and production. Good, solid advice is presented on how to write for diverse audiences in a way that inspires and communicates.

The Exhibition Alliance
EXHIBITIONALLIANCE.ORG
TEA is a nonprofit organization that has served the art exhibition community for more than 40 years by providing comprehensive planning, design and fabrication services. It is a membership cooperative, but many of its services are available to nonmembers. The website offers technical tutorials on budgeting, hardware, measuring light levels and more.

I'd Rather Be in the Studio:
The Artist's No-Excuse Guide
to Self Promotion
by Alyson B. Stanfield
ISBN-13: 978-0-9742-7258-0
Art business consultant Alyson B. Stanfield offers practical information in this book and on her website, artbizcoach.com, for installing and promoting art exhibits.

MRM5-Museum Registration Methods 5th Edition
by Rebecca A. Buck and Jean Allman Gilmore
ISBN: 978-0-8389-1122-2
This new edition of the bible of museum registrars, MRM5 encompasses all that needs to be known about handling and caring for art objects.

The Participatory Museum
by Nina Simon
ISBN-13: 978-0-6153-4650-2
This book is a practical guide to working with community members and visitors to make the exhibition more dynamic, relevant, and essential. The author combines design techniques and case studies to make a powerful case for participatory practice.

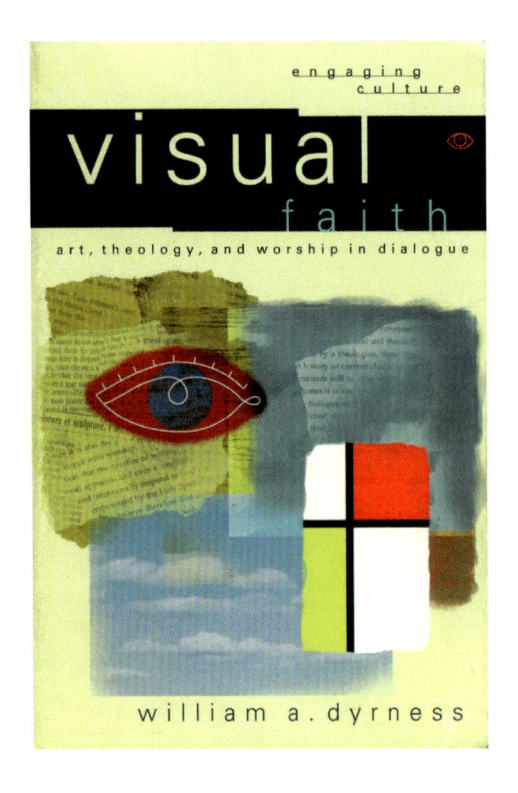

Professional Guidelines
by Harriete Estel Berman
HARRIETE-ESTEL-BERMAN.INFO/
PROFGUIDELINES/PROFGUIDE.HTML
Artist Harriete Estel Berman has generously provided to the arts and crafts community a wide range of documents for professional practices, including condition report, exhibition contract, claims for damaged work and guidelines for working with digital images.

13.3 BOOKS

Art for God's Sake: A Call to Recover the Arts
by Philip Graham Ryken
ISBN: 978-1-5963-8007-3
This booklet addresses foundational issues that Christians face when they seek to intelligently and faithfully engage the visual arts.

Art in Service of the Sacred
by Catherine Kapikian
ISBN: 978-0-6873-5863-2
This combined book and DVD calls congregations to take seriously the role of visual art in worship and in the broader life of the church. It reclaims religious symbols, recovers the role of visual art to engage imaginations, and asserts the importance of the aesthetics of ecclesial space.

Arts Ministry: Nurturing the Creative Life of God's People
by Michael J. Bauer
ISBN: 978-0-8028-6928-9
Through 18 case studies, Bauer lays a solid foundation for arts ministry, grounding it in the historic Christian tradition and urging churches to expand their engagement with creative arts. A concluding chapter explains how to develop an arts ministry.

The Creative Church Handbook: Releasing the Power of the Arts in Your Congregation
by J. Scott McElroy
ISBN: 978-0-8308-4120-2
This book offers practical advice, proven projects and inspirational ideas for congregations interested in bringing more art and creativity into their churches.

Redeeming the Arts: The Restoration of the Arts to God's Creational Intention
FREE DOWNLOAD AT LAUSANNE.ORG

Lausanne Occasional Paper No. 46 was delivered at the 2004 Forum hosted by the Lausanne Committee for World Evangelization. The document followed a two-year long global inquiry that identified the arts as a significant issue for the church in the twenty-first century.

The Substance of Things Seen: Art, Faith, and the Christian Community
by Robin M. Jensen
ISBN-13: 978-0-8028-2796-8

This book is meant to engage church leaders and artists in constructive conversation about the role of art in Christian life and practice.

Visual Faith: Art, Theology, and Worship in Dialogue
by William A. Dyrness
ISBN-13: 978-0-8010-2297-5

Grounded in historical and biblical research, Dyrness offers an intriguing, substantive look into how visual imagery can and should play an important role in modern Christianity.

13.4 ORGANIZATIONS

Calvin Institute of Christian Worship
WORSHIP.CALVIN.EDU

The interdisciplinary ministry center promotes the scholarly study of the theology, history, practice, and renewal of Christian worship in religious communities across North America. It partners with congregations, denominations, and parachurch organizations through events, grants, and by offering practical resources for pastors, church leaders and artists.

CIVA
CIVA.ORG

Christians in the Visual Arts explores and nurtures the relationship of the visual arts and the Christian faith. It produces a broad range of conferences, artist retreats, online networking, podcasts, art exhibits, programs, and publications that help artists, pastors, collectors, critics, designers, art historians, and film makers who work in the intersection of art, faith, and culture.

ECVA
ECVA.ORG

The mission of Episcopal Church and the Visual Arts is to encourage artists and organizations to engage the visual arts in the spiritual life of the church. ECVA values the significance of visual imagery in spiritual formation and faith development. Its website includes an artists registry and art blog.

IFRAA
AIA.ORG/IFRAA

Interfaith Forum on Religion, Art and Architecture, a Knowledge Community of the American Institute of Architects, encourages and supports excellence in the design of worship spaces and their accoutrements. It is a professional association whose primary interest is religious facilities in a broad array of traditions and the exchange of ideas relating to religion, art, and architecture.

Pontifical Council for Culture
CULTURA.VA

This group was founded in 1982 by Pope John Paul II with the aim of establishing dialog between Church and the multiform world of contemporary cultures. Initiatives of the Department of Art and Faith include assistance for artists and promotion of art organizations. The website has a rich archive of resource materials.

13.5 ONLINE

ArtWay
ARTWAY.EU

This web-based service for congregations and individual believers exists to increase understanding of the role of visual arts in deepening faith and worship and communicating truth and hope within culture. Resources include subscription-based weekly visual meditations, profiles of international artists, information about organizations, museums and galleries.

CAELA
CAELA-ARTS.ORG

Christian Arts Entrepreneurs, Leaders and Advocates is an arts service organization providing resources, information and connections for people who are living out their faith in service to God and others through leadership in the arts.

Diary of an Arts Pastor
ARTSPASTOR.BLOGSPOT.COM

Author and theologian David O. Taylor writes "a diary of ruminations and happenings of an arts pastor who never wanted to be a pastor and never thought he could be an artist."

Sacred Art Pilgrim
SACREDARTPILGRIM.COM

This website charts the journey of John A. Kohan, artist and aficionado of modern sacred art. It includes indexes of sacred artists and schools of sacred art, a weekly artist profile, and relevant articles. The site links to Sacred Art Meditations that explores visual themes of sacred art.

Transpositions
TRANSPOSITIONS.CO.UK

The official blog of the Institute for Theology, Imagination and the Arts at University of St. Andrews in Scotland posts articles by notable artists, practitioners and scholars about Christianity and the arts. The website also has an archive of featured artists in different media, resource links and book reviews.

SOURCE CREDITS

SECTION 3.3
"Good Lighting for Museums, Galleries and Exhibitions," Booklet No. 18 in the licht.wissen series Information on Lighting Applications (Frankfurt, Germany: Fördergemeinschaft Gutes Licht, 2000), 6. PDF available at www.en.licht.de/en/info-and-service/publications-and-downloads/lichtwissen-series-of-publications.

SECTION 3.4
Marion F. Mecklenburg and Charles S. Tumosa, "Temperature and relative humidity effects on the mechanical and chemical stability of collections," ASHRAE Journal (April 1999): 69-74.

SECTION 6.3
Beverly Serrell, Exhibit Labels: An Interpretive Approach (Walnut Creek: Alta Mira Press, 1996), 1-7.

SECTION 8.4
Harriete Estel Berman, "Professional Guidelines for the Arts and Crafts Community," Creative Commons Attribution 4.0 International License, 2010. PDF available at www.harriete-estel-berman.info/profguidelines/profguide.html.

SECTION 9.1
Claire S. Barker, "How to Select Gloves: An Overview for Collections Staff," National Park Service Conserve O Gram, September 2010. PDF available at www.nps.gov/museum/publications/conserveogram/01.pdf.

SECTIONS 9.2–9.5
Rebecca A. Buck and Jean Allman Gillmore, MRM.5: Museum Registration Methods, 5th Edition (Washington DC: American Association of Museum Press, 2010), 9-18.

SECTIONS 10.1–10.2
Alyson B. Stanfield, How to Curate and Install Your Art Exhibit Like a Pro (CD-book distributed at workshop by Stanfield Art Associates, Inc., 2008), 6-7. Available through www.artbizcoach.com.

SECTION 10.3
J. Jason Horejs, "How to Hang a Painting: A Guide for Collectors, Artists and Galleries," Creative Commons Attribution 3.0 Unported License (Phoenix, AZ: Red Dot Press and Scottsdale, AZ: Xanadu Gallery, 2013), 8-9. PDF available at http://reddotblog.com/how-to-hang-a-painting-a-free-guide-from-xanadu-gallery.

SECTION 10.4
Mickie McCormick, "Measuring Light Levels for Works on Display," Exhibition Alliance Technical Note (Hamilton, NY: The Exhibition Alliance, 2001). PDF available at www.exhibitionalliance.org/learn/technical-briefs.

SECTION 11.1
Serrell, 22, 30, 33.

SECTION 11.2
Stanfield, 23.

IMAGE CREDITS

IMAGES FOR THIS PROJECT WERE SUPPLIED BY:

Arts of the Covenant in Menlo Park, CA
Berenice Kuiper Rarig
Bowden Collections
CIVA | Christians in the Visual Arts
First Presbyterian Church in Hilton Head, SC
John Knox Presbyterian Church in Seattle, WA
Lincoln Berean Church in Lincoln, NE
Manresa Gallery in San Francisco, CA
Seeds Fine Art Exhibits
Square Halo Gallery in Lancaster, PA
Sojourn Arts and Culture in Louisville, KY
VAM Gallery in Austin, TX
Wilshire Baptist Church in Dallas, TX
Wheatland Presbyterian Church in Lancaster, PA
White Stone Gallery in Philadelphia, PA

ACKNOWLEDGEMENTS

Producing this handbook was a lot like curating and hanging a gallery exhibit. We sought the finest content from the finest creators and we believe we have produced a worthy exhibit. We are deeply grateful for the generous gifts of time and sage advice from the wonderful people who manage church art galleries across the country, especially Patrick Almonrode, Joyce Grimm, Dan Hammer, Mary Ellen Johnson, Rodney Allen Schwartz, Ann Williams, Mark Wingfield, and Michael Winters.

The draft revisions suggested by participants in the "Planning and Developing Church Galleries and Exhibits" workshop at the Calvin Symposium on Worship helped and encouraged us. If we have succeed in communicating current museum standards for art display, we are indebted to Dayton Castleman and Kenneth Steinbach who kindly provided their professional insights.

We owe enormous gratitude for the contributions of our awesome CIVA team: graphic designer, Ned Bustard; web designer, Barry Sherbeck; and marketing maven, Margot Rogers. We are beholden to our editor Cameron Anderson for his patience, guidance, and attention to product design.

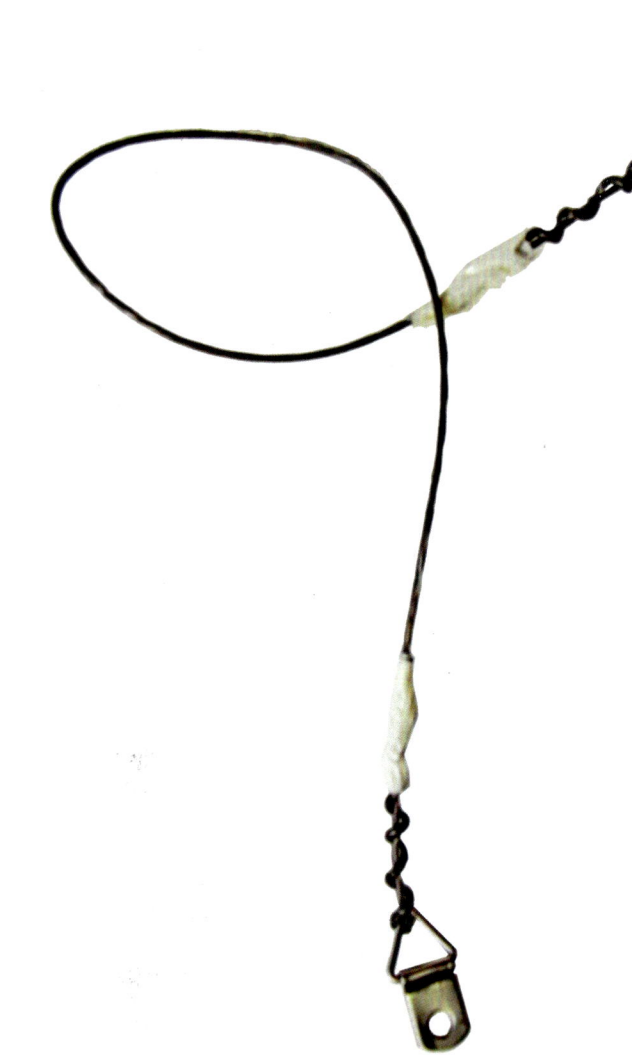

ABOUT THE AUTHORS

Sandra Bowden is an artist, collector, and curator. She has spent the greater part of her career helping churches become more involved in the visual arts. She served on the CIVA Board of Directors for 32 years, and was one of the founders of the Museum of Biblical Art in New York City. Her work is in many collections including Cincinnati Museum, Billy Graham Center Museum, and Vatican Museum of Contemporary Religious Art. Ms. Bowden owns a dozen art exhibits that travel to museums, churches, and educational institutions throughout the country. She has co-written and edited several books, including *Faith and Vision: Twenty-Five Years of Christians in the Visual Arts,* and is featured in *Objects of Grace: Conversations on Creativity and Faith* and *The Art of Sandra Bowden.*

Marianne Lettieri is a studio artist and art instructor who has a background in marketing communications and non-profit arts management. Throughout her life, she has worked at the intersection of art and faith by producing liturgical dance, creative workshops, and art exhibitions for religious venues. Her artwork is in the collections of Oracle Corporation, San Jose Museum of Quilts and Textiles, and City of Palo Alto, California. Ms. Lettieri is the Vice President of CIVA and founder of Arts of the Covenant, an organization for visual artists in the San Francisco Bay Area. She serves on the organizing team of Doing Good Well, a leadership initiative for young women artists of the Christian faith. She has an M.F.A. in Spatial Arts from San Jose State University and a B.F.A. from the University of Florida.